BLACK YOUTH AND THE JUVENILE JUSTICE SYSTEM

MARYLAND THEOLOGICAL SEMINARY

MASTER'S THESIS

BLACK YOUTH AND THE JUVENILE JUSTICE SYSTEM

BY

REV. DR. ANDRE H. HUMPHREY

authorHOUSE®

AuthorHouse™ LLC
1663 Liberty Drive
Bloomington, IN 47403
www.authorhouse.com
Phone: 1-800-839-8640

Published by AuthorHouse   03/06/2014

ISBN: 978-1-4817-3570-4 (sc)
ISBN: 978-1-4817-3569-8 (e)

Library of Congress Control Number: 2013906309

APPROVAL SHEET

TITLE OF THESIS: BLACK YOUTH AND THE JUVENILE JUSTICE SYSTEM

NAME OF CANDIDATE: REV. DR. ANDRE H. HUMPHREY

IN CANDIDACY FOR: MASTER OF DIVINITY

THESEIS PAPER AND
ABSTRACT APPROVED

DR. GROVES

PROFESSOR

DR. PHILLIPS

PROFESSOR

DR. DOUGLASS WILSON

PROFESSOR

DR. HENRY BOULWARE

PROFESSOR

EDUCATION BASED ON DEGREES OBTAINED

2000 -   Graduated from United Baptist College & Seminary
         Bachelor of Arts Degree in Theology

2001 -   Johns Hopkins University—School of Professional
         Studies in Business Education
         Certificate in Business Administration

2002 -   Maryland Eastern Theological Seminary
         Masters of Religious Education

2003 -   Maryland Eastern Theological Seminary
         Master of Divinity

2005 -   Maryland Eastern Theological Seminary
         Doctrine of Divinity

ACKNOWLEDGEMENTS

I wish first to acknowledge and thank Almighty God for allowing me to remain faithful in all that He has instructed me to do.

I would like to acknowledge the contributions of the young men whose lives are the basis of this research paper. I am so grateful to the young men at the Charles Hickey School for trusting me enough to be able to open up to me when I was their mentor. I sincerely hope by allowing them to show this openness it would in turn, allow other youngsters who find themselves in the same situation a chance to be understood.

I could never begin to express my sincere appreciation to my immediate family; Edith Humphrey (mother), Lawrence Humphrey (father), James Grant (brother), and Cynthia Jefferson (sister), as well as, my aunts and uncles for believing in my constant pursuit to aid those who are lost and can't seem to find their way. Words could not begin to express my gratitude for my loving wife, Yolanda and my daughter Keta, for never failing to provide special support and constant understanding.

I would also like to thank my pastor, Rev. Dr. Herman A. Ford, along with my present and past instructors: Rev. Dr. Henry Boulware, Rev. Alexander, Rev. Dr. Russell Groves, Rev. Timothy Wright, Reaching the Unreachable Board Members, Sis. Regina Curtis, Greenmount Recreation and staff, Sis. Terri Fulp, Sis. Torriane, Dr. Macie O. Tillman, and countless others who have encouraged me and supported me as I press toward the mark

Also, In SPECIAL MEMORY OF - My son

Andre Boone

United States Marine

CONTENTS

INTRODUCTION

For several years, the community and society as a whole have tried to understand the functions of juvenile delinquency and the Juvenile Justice System. The following pages have been written to enhance and broaden the common interest in early intervention involving both parents and children. I hope that these pages will bring understanding of the origin of juvenile offenders.

Although it is considered a norm to associate poverty and race as the leading factors of juvenile delinquency, it is now and always will be an unfair statement; however, just because it is unfair, it does not mean it is entirely untrue. Poverty is more common for children than for any other group in society. There are other factors such as social isolation and economic stress, which have proven to be the two main products of poverty.

We need to stop and remember that the reality of street life for most minors is the pathway to violence and crime, which offers rewards that, offset the risks associated with their negative activities. If a child experiences the risks of street life and what it has to offer firsthand, for example, getting shot, stabbed, or killed, this only reinforces the child's desire for more involvement to the learning of street life. They feel as though they can do better the next time by listening more closely to other delinquent peers and rejecting the advice of others in positions of authority. The negative side to this is that when violence is encouraged and rewarded, it is multiplied in negative actions. When coaxed by their peers in continuing to do wrong, it gives them the feeling of greater acceptance.

In this thesis, you will also find topics that discuss the parental involvement in juvenile delinquency, which includes abandonment, abuse, adoption, drug use and other criminal actions. All of these are contributing factors when we examine aspects of why our children go in the wrong direction.

The purpose of this paper is also to examine the black juvenile delinquent in comparison to other races. There is no doubt that a child from the ghetto will grow up in a social atmosphere that may or may not be important to his or her behavior, especially when the system is perceived by them as unjust. They may either rebel against it or accommodate it to their way of life. Black youth reared in the underclass neighborhoods and confined to social disorganization do not encourage a belief in the fairness of the system or for that matter, the entire system. There are many African American males between the ages of 10-18 in the Juvenile Justice System.

Once we admit that the cycle of juvenile justice occurs because people repeat their past rather than learn from it, we will have gained knowledge of the mystery associated with this ongoing problem.

This paper shows how we can break the cycle of juvenile justice by learning from the past, by being open to the lesson it teaches us regardless of whether those lessons support or threaten our views 'of the present and future. We can break the cycle of juvenile in justice by learning about the actual performance of juvenile justice policies that have aided us in the past, regardless of whether those policies seem rational and acceptable, and most of all whether it makes sense to society.

Who are these Young Black Males?

They are looked upon as the most dangerous group in America between the ages of 14-18 years of age. This age group is expected to increase by more than 30% in the next ten years. We can overlook this enormous mission field or we can be a part of the greatest revival that our youth culture has ever experienced in the history of the world.

Most of the youth who commit crimes suffer from the impact of a broken family, the lack of positive peers, and a cultural epidemic of violence and abandoned morals. The juvenile justice institutions today are filled with youth from urban and rural America. Regardless of where these youths may come from, the majority of them will be going back to their communities, maybe in your own neighborhood. We can choose to discard them and overlook them, but we cannot deny that Jesus Christ died for them as well. We must remember that those who deserve love the least need it the most_

If you really think about it, you would also come to the conclusion, that a great number of the incarcerated youth have never had one single positive adult male in their lives who has cared enough to act as a role model for them. Also, a lot of these youths have a parent with a criminal background. It is very clear that at-risk young people are in desperate need of healthy relationships with adults.

Our approach is more about building relationships with young people than building programs to reach them. The Justice Department reported that nearly 1.5 million American children have a mother or a father in the Federal or State prisons. Out of this number, more than half live at home without their fathers. If we were to examine the current events of crimes committed by young black youth, we would clearly see that there is no stability in the home life. These youth are desperate for family, positive relationships, and Godly influences in their lives.

We can sit back and watch young offenders get caught up in the cycle of becoming liters, or we can intervene today and help them break away from a troubled past and become responsible young adults in society. We must get pass the point of saying and thinking that once bad, always bad. We have the power to change the future, but first we must be willing to act on the present.

There is always time to make things right, but the critical question is when do we start? When we see these young males on television because they have just been arrested by the police for committing a crime, we wonder about their home life. We ask ourselves what kind of childhood did they have that would cause them to do such a thing and we also ask what type of parents they had? One day, we will realize that these young men could be our future doctors, lawyers or politicians. However, until we are willing to make some sacrifices, we will never reap the benefits of what they have to offer society. Some people need to be molded and re-fashioned_ It is not an impossible task, and it is a task that someone has to be committed to performing and not just observing.

Look around you. Look at your young male family members, and realize the fact that at any given time, these precious young ones could be on the next state bus in route to a Juvenile Detention Center. We must keep our focus on our young people of today; sure it requires a little more effort on our part, but in the end, it will be well worth the effort.

Our youth are a very important part of our future, and the care and attention that we give them now will definitely determine their outcome. It will also influence the type of people we are bringing up that will represent our future and generations to follow. We have sat back long enough and watched as our young, people committed every unthinkable crime. Well the time is up and we need to make a change. We need to develop a master plan that will put an end to all the chaos that they are experiencing.

Chapter 1

The Environmental Effects That Play A Significant Part In
The Outcome of These Youth

Family Factors

One of the most reliable indicators of juvenile crime is the staggering amount of fatherless children. The primary role of fathers in our society is to provide economic stability, act as role models, and help to alleviate the stress of mothers.

Marriage has always been the best way to multiply capital with the assumption that the girls from poorer families would better themselves by marrying an upstanding male. Then, of course, there are all those values of "love, honor, cherish, and obey" in the marriage tradition. Probably the most important thing that families impart to their children is the emphasis upon the individual's accountability and responsibility in the form of honesty, commitment, loyalty, respect, and work behavior.

Most of the broken home traditions, for example, show only the weak and trivial effects, such as skipping school or home delinquency. Another area shows only those children from two-parent families who become involved in crime at a young age. In fact, there is more evidence supportive of the idea that a stepparent in the home increases delinquency or that abuse and neglect in fully intact homes **often lead to** a cycle of violence. Also to complicate matters, there are significant gender and race concerns.

Very few conclusions can be reached about the African American males, but evidence suggests that stepparents can be of a benefit to them. The differences have actually shown that the broken home is a less important factor. When we look at juvenile delinquency as a whole as opposed to the higher social class of people, we have a higher amount of troubled youth with deeper physiological problems. Most of the research I found was mixed and there is no clear factor that has been proven to explain the commonality in fatherlessness and crime, but it is certainly unfair to blame single mothers, their parenting skills, or their economic conditions. According to the Dept. of Health and Human Services, statistics prove that our children are abused and neglected severely. The following chart will verify this point. The status that they may have in society is continuing to decrease as it is dwindling down to nothing, and this is inflicting damage in their lives, as well as their family life. Some may look at this as a generational curse we tend to believe and also think that just because the parents of these so-called troubled youth had a hard time growing up, their children will not succeed in life. We think that poverty breeds poverty; that the conditions that we imposed on the earlier generation will be automatically transmitted on today's generation. Please examine for the stats for 2000, which is a strong explanation of why our children should be our priority.

National Fact Sheet 2003

Making Children a National Priority

America's Children At-A-Glance

	Number of Children*
Children referred for possible child abuse and neglect, 2000[1]	2,796,000
Children substantiated or indicated as abused or neglected, 2000[2]	879,000
Children who died as a result of abuse or neglect, 2000[3]	1,236
Children in foster care on September 30, 2000[4]	547,415
Children waiting to be adopted on September 30, 2000[5]	133,057
Grandparents raising grandchildren, 2000[6]	2,431,349
Children who ran away from a foster care placement, 2000[7]	15,811
Children who ran away from home, 1999[8]	1,682,900
Children lacking medical insurance, 2001[9]	8,500,000
Children younger than 6 below the poverty level, 2000[10]	4,000,000

*Number of children estimated

One of the main causes in the constant rise in the number of juvenile delinquency is money. When looking at the overall picture, we will find that a great deal of these offenders originate from low-income families. As far back as we can remember

---

[1] Administration on Children, Youth, and Families (2002). Child Maltreatment 2000. Washington, D.C.: U.S. Department of Health & Human Services.
[2] Ibid.
[3] Ibid.
[4] Ibid.
[5] Ibid.
[6] Ibid.
[7] Ibid.
[8] Ibid.
[9] Ibid.
[10] Ibid.

obtaining money and fair pay has been the number one struggle for the black community.

We have been taught by society that we should grow up to be the responsible adults and that we should maintain our lives a certain way. Blacks are taught that our children should attend the best schools and colleges, get the most profitable jobs, and marry the most upstanding person. However, when this does not happen, what happens to our families, our communities, and our society? The young black male is tired of adjusting to whatever is thrown his way; he is tired of accepting the hand me downs of a socially stuck up society. We can all sit around and continue to talk about a better way of doing things, but until we find the solution, we will continue to be a part of this cycle. How do we tell our young people that we cannot afford to send them to college, that we cannot go on a vacation, that they cannot live in the suburbs, and that we cannot go out to dinner? When does life become fair for our young black males? Harry J. Holzer, Chief Economist at the U. S. Department of Labor, has identified five factors that contribute to these questions, as well as the labor market difficulties experienced by young black men:

"Lower educational attainment, both in years and in quality of education;

Limited early work experience, particularly in the transition from school to work;

Lack of easy access. to employers and jobs, including transportation to suburban jobs, information about jobs, and informal networks with employers;

Labor market discrimination; and

The existence of alternative/illegal sources of income."[11]

Black fathers do not devote ample time to childrearing; they have no idea as to what goes on in the minds of their children. Fathers need to devote more time

---

[11] Harry J. Holzer, Chief Economist, U.S. Department of Labor, testimony before the U.S. Commission on Civil Rights, April 16, 1999.

and effort to the lives which they are responsible for, especially their mail children. According to violent felons found 22-34 percent had imitated crime techniques they watched on television programs and video tapes."[12]

If we were to reexamine history of murders committed by young people, we would find that parents did not have supported evidence of any problems or discourse with their children. Dr. Dewey Cornell, Clinical Psychologist and Professor at the University of Virginia had these words to say: "The third group is most puzzling, because they often appear to be normal youngsters whose acts of violence surprise us. However, these youth are emotionally troubled and conflicted—alienated, angry, and depressed. They may be intelligent and capable, but they are not satisfied with their, achievements and often fell unfairly treated by others. Although they may have some friends, they feel lonely and isolated. They are highly sensitive to teasing and bullying, and are deeply resentful, ruminating over perceived injustices. As they become more depressed, their judgment and perspective becomes distorted, the suicidal person who thinks life isn't worth living and that there is no way to solve their problems other than dying. In this case, however, the conflicted youth decides to kill others rather than himself. These are the youth who are involved in most of the school shootings."[13]

Family support should be the most valuable source of security that these young people rely on. I suggest that we as family-oriented people arrive at workable solutions of how to improve the lives of these so-called lost individuals. Sure, those of us who are Christians know that God will make a way for our young people, but we need to step up to the plate and do what we can as well_ It does take a village

---

[12] David Kopel, *Massing the Medium: Analyzing and Responding to Media Violence Without Harming the First Amendment*, Kansas Journal of Law and Public Policy. March 2000.

[13] D. G. Cornell, *What Works in Youth Violence Prevention.* Charlottesville, VA: Curry School of Education, University of Virginia.

to raise one child, and thatappetite for becoming involved with violence; and it frequently shows how often the things that they want can be obtained through the use of aggression and violence. Extensive viewing of television violence also by children causes greater aggressiveness. Sometimes watching a single violent program can increase aggressiveness. Children, who are left alone to watch television shows where violence is so realistic, are more likely to imitate what they see, due to the fact that most children view television as realistic to everyday life.

The impact of television violence may be immediately evident in a child's behavior or may surface years later. Young people can even be affected when the family atmosphere shows no tendency toward violence; however, this does not mean that violence on television is the only source for aggressive or violent behavior, but it is a significant contributor. Television is being blamed for children becoming violent in later life because it is any easy scapegoat.

In many families, televisions are placed in the child's room to act as an electronic baby-sitter; a replacement for quality time with parents_ The Kaiser Family Foundation states that "99 percent of American homes have at least one television; 53 percent of children ages 2 to 18 have a TV in their bedroom, which allows for unsupervised viewing."[14] These children will find themselves learning behaviors not from their parents, but from television. Sexual violence in X- and R-rated videotapes widely available to teenagers has also been shown to cause and increase male anger against females. David Kopel, in Massing the Medium: Analyzing and Responding to Media Violence Without Harming the First Amendment, stated that "Young American maleRonald Rohner, "Having a loving and nurturing father was as important for a child's happiness, well-being, and social and academic success as having a loving and nurturing mother. Withdrawal of love by either the father or the

---

[14]   Kaiser Family Foundation, *Kids & Media @ the New Millennium* (Nov. 1999): 9, 12.

mother was equally influential in predicting a child's emotional instability, lack of self-esteem, depression, social withdrawal, and level of aggression."[15]

We as parents need to take the time and investigate the music they listen to, the activities they participate in, the social circles they travel in and the directions that our Young people are involved in. After consideration of several research findings, it is my conclusion that heavy exposure to televised violence is one of the significant causes of violence in society.

Joy D. Osofsky, in her article, *Children in a Violent Society* says, "It is estimated that today's children will be exposed to approximately twenty to twenty-five violent acts per hour during a Saturday morning and approximately five violent acts per hour during the regular adult programming. Viewing television violence may lead to a change in the child's value and an increase in violent behavior. Television desensitizes the child to violence in general and to the pain of others. If children are "glued" to the television for a substantial portion of their days, they may view the world as more dangerous than it really is.[16]

Viewing violence on the television screen has the following negative effects: it increases the minor's fear of becoming a victim of violence, with a resultant increase in self-protective behaviors and increased mistrust of others; it increases the viewer'sone child can make a difference in the lives of others. Who are these young men? They are our future.

The family structure sets the ground rules for the upbringing of young people. If the family is always contending with abuse, domestic battering, and other behavioral problems, these characteristics will be imparted to the children. It is not easy for them to cope with or understand how to handle such problems. They only imitate

---

[15] Ronald P. Rohner and Robert A Veneziano, *The Importance of Father Love: History and Contemporary Evidence.* Review of General Psychology 5.4 (December 2001): 382-405.

[16] Joy D. Osofsky, *Children in a Violent Society.* New York: Guilford Press, 1997.

what they have been accustomed to seeing. The problem is that we as parents have failed to provide a well-rounded description of what life is supposed to be about. Families arc not all to blame. We also have other sources such as the total environment. Our surroundings play a vital role as well as the family. Once a child leaves the home, he/she is on their own to deal with the day-to-day problems and sometimes this will trigger violence, attitude problems, social problems, and coping in general.

Families that experience such problems should be willing. to seek help from professional agencies to assist them in providing or promoting responsible behavior among all family members. They could also assist them in developing skills to more effectively manage their children's negative behaviors. It seems as though it is a timeless effort and a training effort to seek solutions to prevent juvenile delinquency. We need to step back and realized the fact that we as a generation have failed our young people. We need to seek effective steps to juvenile prevention.

In their article, *Behavioral Family Interventions for Improving Childrearing: A Review of the Literature for Clinicians and Policy Makers,* T. K. Taylor and A. Biglan, stated, "There are several well-conducted random studies of the effects of intervention in early infancy to improve parenting in high-risk groups of different kinds, especially lowbirth weight infants. Such as Parent and family Based Strategy, Home Visiting Strategy, Social-Cognitive Strategy, and mentoring Strategy. The effectiveness of parenting interventions seems to increase exponentially when children are very young, before antisocial or aggressive behaviors are fully developed. By the time child reaches adolescence, both the child and the parents are following well-established pattern and are more resistant to long-terin change."[17]

---

[17] T. K. Taylor and A. Biglan., *Behavioral Family Interventions for Improving Childrearing*: *A Review of the Literature for Clinicians and Policy Makers.* Clinical Child and Family Psychology Review 1998; (1): 41-60.

In their article, *Boy's Behavioral Inhibition and Risk of Later Delinquency*, M. Kerr, R.E. Tremblay, L. Pagnai-Kuit, and F.Vitaro, say, "Typically, home visiting nurses provide guidance on infant development, home care generally, and parenting skills in particular. These findings have been reasonably consistent in showing substantial benefits in relation to the prevention of child abuse and neglect, improved cognitive development, and reduced behavioral difficulties. The findings have obvious implications with respect to the possibility of preventing delinquency in the offspring."[18]

Racial Conflicts and the Juvenile Justice System

In the Baltimore Sun, T. Richissin stated in his column entitled Race Predicts Handling of many Young Criminals . Care vs. Punishment of Mentally III Youth Correlates with Color, "That, research conducted in Maryland revealed that Black children are sent to juvenile jails whereas White children with similar mental disorder, offenses, criminal histories, and mental health problems are placed in residential treatment centers. The Maryland Juvenile Justice Coalition specifically noted that in1998, '120 White juveniles were sentenced to treatment in Maryland's residential centers and 223 White juveniles were jailed. At the same time, 132 Black juveniles received treatment while 672 were confined with no treatment."[19]

The over-representation of youth of color in juvenile confinement continues to soar in direct proportion. Some researchers have found that the higher rate of incarceration is largely due to the higher number of crimes committed by youth; however, incarceration rates are not an effective and exact measure of criminal

---

[18]   M. Kerr, R.E. Tremblay, L. Pagnai-Kuit, & F. Vitaro, *Boy's Behavioral Inhibition and Risk of Later Delinquency.* (1997). Archives of General Psychiatry, 54, 809-16.

[19]   T. Richissin, *Race Predicts Handling of Many Young Criminals: Care vs. Punishment of Mentally Ill Youth Correlates with Color.* The Baltimore Sun, (June 25, 1999), p_ 1A.

activity among African Americans. Such findings fail to recognize the prevalent racial disparities that cause poor minorities to be arrested because of a self-fulfilling prophecy. This to me suggests that minorities are more prone to participate in criminal activities. Please do not be offended by this last statement as it is not intended to downplay the black male; however, given the circumstances when one examines the underlying facts, the young black males have always been the ones labeled as troublemakers and gang bangers.

It is time we change our image and the way others perceive us. One of the main causes of failure in any circumstance is the lack of knowledge. For so long the black man has accepted whatever he was taught or told. No matter what the outcome, he accepted it as his fate. In today's society, we as a people need to read and study about those things that affect our everyday existence. In doing so, the courts, judges and the lawyers will see that we can no longer be called the "ignorant generation."

We must also change the thinking of the court system by educating ourselves on what the current laws are and how they play a role in the black man's life. People have a strong tendency to take advantage of the weaker individual. A poor uneducated blackman with a limited amount of education will be appointed a lawyer by the court to handle his defense and that same lawyer will get him to admit guilt or accept a lesser charge. Now on the other hand, if this same man knew his legal rights and was current on the laws pertaining to his own case, the court officials— would be slow to take advantage of him.

Community Centers: What Do They Have to Offer?

When we look at the overall scope or picture of our young black youth and the environment' that they are reared, we find very few community based programs. The government can find various ways to spend the taxpayer's money; however, to put these monies back into the community is simply a forgotten issue. Through my Outreach Ministry, **I** have found that most of the children who are given a positive outlet are less likely to commit serious crimes. Society has deemed our youth as the new Generation X, the unknown generation, the generation without a purpose, the generation that shows no fear and no remorse for its actions_ If this same society would open its doors of opportunity to these individuals, they would clearly see the positive side, the side that would produce intelligent resourceful adults to aid and uplift the community_

The YMCA Youth & Family Services support and strengthen individual and family life. The services provided help abused children, troubled youth and families in crisis. Project service areas include:

- Prevention and treatment of child abuse
- Shelter care for troubled adolescents
- Prevention of violence/gang activity/drug abuse
- Independent living skills training/job training
- Family life education and counseling/teen pregnancy

YMCA Youth and Family Services help to instill leadership and character, self-esteem and respect.

There are various organizations that could assist in community-based programs, (e.g., the church). The time has come that the church stepped up and became accountable for what is happening in their communities. With any organization, it is highly critical that we first seek to establish programs that are committed to helping our juveniles. There are so many people who desire to have a program, but when it comes down to actually stepping in and becoming a physical asset, many of us find that this is too hard to accomplish. Sure we can provide monetary support and that would be greatly appreciated, but the young people need physical bodies, people that are willing to go that extra mile. These children need to physically see that adults do Care about helping them to—achieve their goals. They also need to see that we can build programs and not, just detention centers_

There are never too many ideas or suggestions when we address the youth. All of us know how short their attention span can be; they seem to bore very easily. Therefore, if each community could come up with at least 10 dedicated people and provide some type of service to keep them interested in obtaining their goals, the program would surely succeed along with the blessings of our Lord and Savior.

There are so many obstacles that are being presented to our youth on a daily basis. We as leaders must step in and become the important part of these youngsters' lives. Outside of God, they need to know that there are people and organizations that they can reach out to, and gain support and strength, also the tools in which they need to survive. There is no better way to establish this than in the church.

The young people of today's society are crying out for love, as well as attention and directional focus. They feel the need to be reassured of the positive decisions that they are faced with making be it in school, home life, or in social atmospheres. The youth of today are ambitious, zealous and lack guidance and direction. Young people have the tendency to resist what they are made to do. In other words, be open enough to listen to what the young people are interested in; just do not assume their way of thinking is your way of By all means, if you are going to start a community based activity, please have the compassion and opened-mindedness to include the teenagers in whatever project that concerns them. This way, you have vital input from both sides of the fence.

Concerns of the School System and Classmates

Violence prevention programs work when they are properly executed. In order for any set of rules to work they must be established and implemented with the full participation, as well as, the support of teachers, board members, parents, students and community members. The following is a list of those opportunities:

1. Establish a working relationship with schools.

Educators, police, and juvenile justice authorities all play an integral part in preventing school crime. Educators are better equipped to the teach students and the police are more capable of intervening in a crisis situation involving a violent or potentially violent student. Juvenile' justice authorities can assign probation officers and social workers to schools, where they can better monitor and serve students, design specific regimens for youthful offenders to influence their behavior, and provide stronger and broader sanctions for violent behavior.

2. Patrol the school grounds, facilities, and travel routes.

The presence of police in or near the school and local neighborhoods deters crime and prevents troubling situations from escalating.—Police presence disrupts trouble spots that interfere with students traveling to and from school, prevents strangers from entering schools, reduces the ability of students to smuggle weapons into schools, deters gang activities, and identifies students who are selling drugs or under the influence of drugs. Police can also conduct random searches for weapons or controlled substances, if appropriate. In these and other circumstances, they add their broader authority to the supervision of students.

3. Respond to reports of criminal activities in the school.

When police routinely patrol the school grounds, they are in a better position to act quickly in response to a request for help from school authorities_ The role of police in this situation may be to separate a violent study **from** potential victims, talk the student into giving up a threatening stance, subdue and transport a student from the scene, contact emergency services, assist in traffic control as emergency services arrive and as parents pick up their children during or after a crisis, collect evidence, or participate in other activities. Rapid response is critical in a situation where many children are in harm's way.

4. Consult with school authorities and parents regarding school security.

Both juvenile justice authorities and police have specialized training in working with youth. They are aware of effective techniques for modifying the behavior of troubled students, the appropriate use of rules and sanctions for youth who are chronic offenders, techniques for avoiding violence and victimization, and optional programs and services for troubled student& They are also able to consult more broadly on issues of school, home, and personal security. Their information can be shared in school board meetings, community meetings, staff meetings, classrooms, assemblies, printed materials, and broadcasts_

5. Work directly with youth to maintain a constructive relationship.

Police and juvenile justice authorities can become involved directly with students outside the police station, courtroom, or other corrective settings. They often develop a good relationship with students as a means of preventing a confrontation in the future.

Those youth who come in contact with the police for non-violent crimes may be place under informal supervision (not taken to jail). The police may make the decision of routinely checking up on the individual. They can all make deals with juvenile offenders and their parents. Freedom from official action may be granted in some situations by voluntary commitment to a public or private program that has people-changing goals.

The U.S. Department of Labor states in the Occupational Outlook Handbook, that "Many people who are convicted of crimes are placed on probation instead of being sent to prison. During probation, offenders must stay out of trouble and meet various requirements. Probation officers, who also may be referred to as community supervision officers in some states, supervise people who have been placed on probation."[20]

Opportunities for building constructive relationships between authorities and youth can include bicycle registration drives, school carnivals, fundraisers, community policing partnerships, and sponsored recreational activities.

Parental Concerns

Every parent is faced with the question of, "What will my child grow up to be?" We can only hope that we have done our best in raising responsible adults. Unfortunately, we have families that despite every possible warning at least one of their children will end up in the juvenile justice system. Society says that the family structure is greatly linked to the social behavior of a child. In other words,

---

[20] Bureau of Labor Statistics, *Occupational Outlook Handbook, 2002-03 Edition,* Probation Officers and Correctional Treatment Specialists. U.S. Department of Labor.

the emotional stress that a child feels regarding his family will most likely be acted out in other areas of his/her life. Families who are unable to communicate with each other create avenues of depression, denial and rejection. All of these leave emotional scars and cause trauma in an adolescent's life. In his book, *American Youth Violence,* Frank Zirnring says, "Many young people who become involved in violence come from families in which there is a long history of domestic violence_ Many young people who are violent have been raised in homes that have been, if not technically abusive, hostile and conflict-ridden."[21]

The question posed is should we hold the parents responsible for the actions of a minor? The answer is yes. If the judge would require the parents of the offender to appear in the Juvenile Court, he would have the opportunity of reinforcing warnings to the parents. It would allow 'the judge to see firsthand the family environment of the offender. Too many times the parents are not willing to show up in court as many times as required by the judge. They get in the habit of sending someone to represent them or they put too much confidence in legal representation.

Most juvenile delinquents started out as good kids with little or no attention and involvement from their working parents. Sooner or later, these same children found themselves in bad situations. They made choices that were not positive and meaningful for their lives. They longed for attention and love, and they became willing to do most anything to obtain it. A female looking for love from her father will go to an outside man for that same love, and unfortunately, she will be mistreated in some cases. Regardless of a parent's best effort, minors can be coached and influenced by peer pressures and they are quick to pick up bad habits outside of the home. We as parents must learn to recognize the telltale signs that our precious

---

[21]   Franklin E. Zincing, *American Youth Violence.* New York: Oxford University Press, 1998_

little ones are involved in activities that are less likely to be desired. These activities might be anything from gangs, guns, drug abuse, stealing, and yes, even murder.

When establishing rules for children, it is important for parents to communicate their views on crime, violence, weapons, and appropriate self-defense. Children also need to know that parents support school discipline policies and any reasonable punishments that are administered by the school. Children should understand the rationale for household, school, and other rules and behavioral expectations. If a child misbehaves, punishments may be more effective if they are consistent and appropriate to the severity and frequency of the offense and administered with a gentle' voice and with full explanation.

Discipline means more than punishment. Involving children in activities that teach constructive skills such as responsibility, appropriate play behavior, self-control, and goal setting is as important as sanctioning them for inappropriate behavior. Parents can devise rewards and incentives for good behavior to prevent future rule violations and to urge constructive behaviors.

One of the best ways to teach a child is by demonstration. Through their everyday actions, parents teach their children how to interact socially, handle competition and defeat, discuss differences, resolve conflicts, deal with frustration in solving problems, and cope with stress and anger, among other skills. Children also learn from the other adults in their. lives and may require help understanding different behavior responses to similar challenges. Their inevitable exposure to negative influences makes the parent's role as a model of behavior even more important.

Get involved with school and community organizations and activities. Becoming active in the child's school and community life brings many benefits. It provides parents the opportunity to see more of what the child sees, therefore gaining a deeper understanding of the child's needs. Situations arise that present opportunities for reinforcing what is taught in the home. The presence of parents provides continuity for the student in moving from one setting to another. Being involved also gives parents an opportunity to get to know teachers, childcare providers, and coaches, among others, and to work with them to ensure that the child's needs are met when parents are not present_ A program entitled F.A.S.T. (Families and Schools Together) is one avenue that has been successful at involving low-income, stressed, and isolated parents in dealing with their troubled youth. FAST has a statistically significant positive impact on children and families, it works with school teachers to identify elementary school children about whom they have development or behavioral concerns.

Let's take time to examine some of the telltale signs of minors headed for Juvenile Detention Centers.

Gangs

Gang activities are the cause of serious problems in the community, but it is a terrible opponent to your child. Minors who are involved in gangs become criminals and sometimes they become victims of violent crimes. If all of a sudden your child comes home one day and he/she is wearing unfamiliar clothing with a certain color scarf tied around his/her head, you know that kind of action is out of the ordinary. Better still, some telltale signs could be if your child shows a lack of interest in school, fights, stays out late, acquires strange body piercing, tattoos, hangs out with kids you know are definitely gang members. Gang Researchers have examined the influence of peers through a variety of measures, including exposure to delinquent peers, attachment to delinquent peers, and commitment to delinquent peers. According to S. Battin, K.G. 1-till and R. Catalano, "Regardless of how this peer affiliation is measured, the results are the same: association with delinquent peers is one of the strongest predictors (this is, risk factors) of gang membership."[22] All of these are signs of danger and they must be addressed immediately if we ever want to save our children and our communities. Gang members may commit a significant number of crimes, but crime is often not their primary and certainly not their only focus. Youth often join gangs to achieve goals that they perceive as difficult or impossible to achieve without gang support. Most of these gang members are adolescent or young adult males. Therefore, we as parents need to take control of the situation, we need to get involved and stay involved.

Stealing

Let's face the facts, we know what we can and cannot afford for our children. Sure we would like to give them the world and all the glamour that goes along with it, but it is time that we wake up. There are certain things we will never be able to do. When your child comes home with expensive tennis shoes, clothing and jewelry, and you know that you did not give them the money for these items, and you know he/she does not have a job, there should be no hesitation in our actions or responses. It is time we question our children, even if it is invading their privacy. Too many times we ignore the obvious.

If we were to ask the children who are caught stealing, "why did they do it?" They would more or less say, "I do not know." The reasons are because they are so angry, depressed, or confused, and that they truly believe that this type of act will allow them to release all of the pressures that they have inside. They also do these things to gain attention from their parents; they feel that they have to do wrong before they are noticed.

---

[22]   S. Baran, K.G. Abbott and R. Catalano, *Criminology*. 1998. 36(1): 93-115.

We are so quick to say that our children are not capable of committing such acts that we fail to deal with what is in our very own face. Peer pressure is something that will never go away, no matter how much we try to reassure our children. They will continue to want those things that they do not have. Sometimes I think they shoplift just for the fun of it; it is more or less a game to them. They think that they will never get caught. Stealing is a serious crime and the consequences are serious as well. If parents become liable for their children's actions and they are made to pay restitution by the court, maybe then we will have less offenders of this crime.

Just like drugs, anything can become an addiction. The parents that allow stolen saying that it is okay to steal. They are saying that it is okay to take what does not belong to, you.

Once our children fall into this category, we must do everything in our power to help them. There are many organizations that deal with problems such as stealing and shoplifting that are all too willing to save our young people. Once we allow this crime to go unnoticed, we are only setting ourselves up for later discomfort. The children that were once labeled as shoplifters are now our adults; the very same people that we trust alone in our homes; and the very same people that we employ. Now, they are not only stealing a pack of gum or lipstick, they are stealing millions of dollars; they are vandalizing our homes and property; they are causing the prices to be raised in our neighborhood stores. The more they steal, the more we end up paying back in the long run.

Weapons

The youth today have too many ways of obtaining illegal firearms, more now than ever before. If we were to look back in time, we cannot recall a time where the rate of youth committing offenses with guns had reached such a record breaking level. Years ago, there was no such thing as gun restriction. You could purchase a gun just about in any store that carried them. It is not the sale of guns that have gone out of control, but the negative use that is out of control. Juveniles who carry a weapon are more likely to have been involved in a prior confrontation than those who did not carry a weapon. Although many youth feel that carrying a weapon is helpful in avoiding a fight; however, the presence of a weapon increases the likelihood of violence and/or injury. Communities can reduce the number of handguns within their borders by reporting to the police those minors who have these illegal weapons in their possession. There are often time dreadful results behind youth and gun. The Centers for Disease Control and Prevention produced a report which says, "Although guns kill more White children than Black children, young Black males are particularly affected by gun violence. Homicide is the leading cause of death among Black males ages 15 to 24, and the firearm death rate for Black males 15-19 is four times that of White males of the same age."[23]

Our young people see violence on a day-to-day basis. When the television is turned on, someone is always being robbed, raped, or killed, and a gun is almost always involved in the scenario. Everyday on the news, someone somewhere is the victim of a violent crime, again involving a gun. These are children killing children and the sad part is that they do realize the extent of their actions. They have no moral standard on which to base their conduct and their actions_ They have abandoned the positive guidelines set by their parents. There is no reason why a child should fear going to school because they are fearful of losing their life_ It is unthinkable what society has allowed to happen to our young people. They no longer read books or have family outings on the weekend; instead they buy them all of the latest video games and, sit them in front of the television. The media has been given the job

---

[23] Centers for Disease Control and Prevention, *National Vital Statistics Reports, Vol. 48, No. 11. Table 8.* July 2000.

of raising our children. It has been given the job of being our baby-sitters, our mediators and, finally our substitute parents.

We no longer teach our children to talk things over and work out their misunderstandings_ Instead, we advise them not to allow anyone to walk over them and to stand up and be a man/woman. Well that is all fine and good, but when they steal their parent's gun and take matters into their own hands and someone else's child is hurt or killed, the parent is quick to say, "Why didn't you come to me?" We are living in days where the young people have no fear or respect for anyone. The so-called good children are being forced to defend themselves. You can take a child that never gets into confrontations with their peers, always studies and does his/her best, and that same child because of daily pressure will snap back and do the unexpected.

The following chart from the 1999 National Report produced by Kids and Guns, gives evidence of the growing number of homicides committed by teenage boys both black and white. [24]

---

[24] *ile Offenders and Victims: 1999 National Report.*

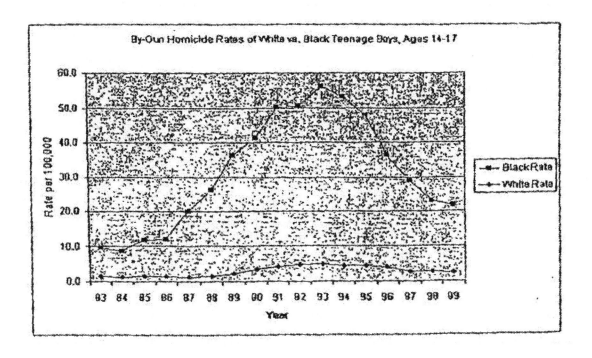

There are certainly laws that are supposed to govern the sale of firearms but these laws are not enough. I say this because we have too many people out there just thinking of ways to make money and have no morals about how they obtain their finances. You can always go to someone who is willing to break the law. There are too many negative resources available to our young people. It is a constant battle between the court system, politicians, and parents on what really benefits the young people of today. In 1994, the State of Maine enacted a law that allows youths more than 10 years of age to possess firearms when hunting if they are accompanied by a parent or another adult approved by a parent or guardian_ [25] This is the prime example of giving youth the opportunity to handle firearms. Sure they learn to hunt animals, and they learn to be perfect shooters. Once they have mastered shooting animals, what will prevent them from taking a gun to school and shooting their classmates and teacher? Better still when they are angered by parents what will

---

[25] ME. R_ev. State Ann. Title 12, 7101(a), (West Supp. 1196).

stop them from turning the gun on them? Or, if this child becomes depressed what prevents them from taking his own life? There is no evidence to support the idea that minors should have guns. One strategy of reducing these high firearm-related death rates among youngsters is to limit their access to firearms by raising the age limit for firearm ownership. First, this will reduce the success of suicide attempts because the lethality of firearms means that a cry for help by a youngster results in death more often when a firearm is used.

The statistics on youth suicide are similar to those for murder: for every two murders, there is one suicide_ These suicides are committed mostly in the teen years (95%), mostly by males (80%), and mostly by way of firearms (67%). U.S_ youth homicide and suicide rates far exceed those for other economically developed nations. The U.S. youth homicide rate is five times the number of the typical Western European nation (2.57 per 100,000 children versus 0.51), while youth homicides involving firearms is 16 times greater. The pattern is the same for suicide: the U.S. rate is twice the rate of other developed countries (0.55 versus 0.27), and 11 times the rate for suicides involving firearms.[26] Second, research has shown that the social characteristics of victims (age, race and gender) are often very similar to that of perpetrators. This means that the perpetrators of gun homicides are very often young themselves, thus raising the age limit for gun ownership will exclude many of these youngsters from owning a firearm, and so being able to easily kill another young person by pulling a trigger.

Because firearm-related injuries tend to be more severe than other types of injuries, they are more difficult and expensive to treat. As the number of gun-related injuries decline, so will the cost of treatment. This will have a significant impact

---

[26] *Accessibility of Firearms and the Use of Firearms By or Against Juveniles.* Office of Juvenile Justice and Delinquency Prevention, U.S. Department of Justice. Washington, D.C. 2000.

on reducing the cost of gun violence, particularly as many patients cannot afford the resulting fees, which means the state bears most of the cost for firearm injuries, including expensive surgery. Less gun violence incidents will mean that the burden on the criminal justice system will be lightened, by the lack of cases to investigate and prosecute. Limiting the access youngsters have to firearms by raising the age limit for firearm ownership will also significantly reduce the human cost of gun violence. Any gun injury is traumatic for the victim and his/her family but when the victim is a young person who still has his/her whole life ahead of them, the trauma is especially marked. It used to be that parents expected to die before their children, but the prevalence of gun violence among young people in America has meant that many children are dying before their parents. Often parents of gun violence victims are often expected to care for their child, instead of the child caring for them in their old age.

Most youth who become involved with guns acquire their first firearm in early adolescence. According to a report by Snyder and Siclcmund, "Many adolescents own and use guns legally for sporting activity, but there is a perception that an increasing number of other adolescents own guns for protection and carry them on the street. In fact, one study of urban juvenile arrestees found that more than two-thirds of the juveniles said their primary reason for owing and carrying a weapon was self-protection; a smaller number also reported using their weapon for drug trafficking or other illegal activity. It is illegal gun ownership and use among adolescents that constitute a problem of great concern. Researchers and policymakers have become increasingly interested in understanding patterns of gun ownership and use among adolescents so that programs can be developed to respond to this problem."[27]

---

[27] H.N.Snyder and M.. Sickrnund, *Juvenile Offenders and Victims: 1999 National Report.* Washington, D.C.: U.S. Department of Justice, Office of Justice Programs, Office of

Most receive their first gun from someone else, whether this is a parent giving a child his first hunting rifle as a Christmas gift, or a teenager giving his best friend an illegally acquired handgun for protection. By middle to later adolescence when delinquent boys are more likely to be arrested, they have begun to actively obtain handguns from a variety of sources, including buying from a drug dealer or an adult "straw purchaser," (a term used for an adult who aides a child in obtaining drugs) borrowing from a friend or acquaintance, burglary, or theft. If we hope to intervene to reduce juvenile gun violence, it is important to understand what motivates youth at three key points in the chain of events that precedes almost every shooting. The first is the decision to acquire a handgun; second, the decision to carry it; and finally, the decision to use it.

Juvenile Justice and Delinquency Prevention.

Chapter 2

The Economic Background of Typical Black Inner City Families with Troubled Youths

An Overview of Children Reared in Low Income Areas

We tend to question ourselves everyday as to whether or not the area in which we live has an influence on our children and their well-being. Years ago when **I was** growing up, the only influence you had was that of your parents. They instilled good and valuable morals and ethics_ The values that they had were vital if you were to succeed in life_ Everyone in the community had a hand in raising the neighborhood children. Today, there is so much confusion and discord in the corrununity that parents remain fearful all the time It is unthinkable to send your child to the store, or even allow them to play outside because of the level of violence surrounding them on a daily basis. However, the more we examine the number of crimes the more we **find that it** is happening in the "rich" areas, as well as the poverty stricken areas. We cannot **continue to put a label on** certain areas and deeming them the" Vicirtrones in which to raise a child. It is not the "area" or "environment". It is, however, the people who live in those areas. Some of the most heinous crimes are committed in the suburbs; the sections where the upper class of people reside. Their children are the ones who cross over into the city limits in order to purchase drugs and commit crimes. Their children are the ones who come from two parent families, two car garages, and single-family homes. One of the reasons is because they believe they can get away with anything. They also believe their parents can buy their way out of a bad situation.

There is no general pattern or framework that we can pinpoint to dismiss the dim future of our neglected youth. We can exchange all of the theories and scientific findings we like, but the fact still remain that the struggle will continue unless we contribute more to the growth and quality of our own well-being. There are so many factors that assist as well as hinder our young people. In an article entitled, "The At Risk Youth Industry," published *in The Atlantic Monthly,* Jennifer Washburn stated that "13 million American children were living in poverty, three million more than in 1979."[28] This was done as a study at Columbia University.

The chart below outlines a breakdown of the dropout rates from grades 10 through 12 and number of distribution among 15-24 year-olds, by background characteristics:

Characteristic	Even dropout rate%	Number of even dropouts (thousands)
Total	4.8	488
Sex		
Male	5.5	280
Female	4.1	208
Race/ethnicity		
White, non-Hispanic	4.1	276
Black, non-Hispanic	6.1	91
Family Income		
Low Income	10.0	141
Middle Income	5.2	298
High Income	1.6	48
Age		
15 – 16	2.9	84
17	3.5	121
18	6.1	165

---

[28] Jennifer Washburn, *The At Risk Youth Industry.* The Atlantic Monthly, December 2002.

They feel at an early age that there is no sense of trying to succeed educationally because they are never going to have what their white counterparts possess. This has been prevalent ever since the days of slavery. Fortunately, it is time for us to move forward_ It is not the place where we live, the clothes that we wear or the car that we drive that defines us, and it is definitely not our past. It is our drive and determination, our perception of a better way of life that determines our future and the future of our youth. We must tirelessly continue to express the need for education when we address the young people of today. It is a disturbing thing to come to the realization that so many of them cannot read or write, and that they will not be able to survive in this world without the proper level of education.

Pressures of Young Black Males

Gender has always played a significant part in the African American household. It is a known fact that blacks have very different and unique problems and priorities. They have to overcome certain issues in regards to race on a daily basis_ African-American males contend with problems of high unemployment rates, drug abuse, crime, and certainly lack of sufficient education; however, the male's role has always been to take care of the needs of their families. This way of thinking has diminished due to the lack of male representation in. the black family, which has been replaced by women who struggle to raise children in single parent homes. This has strongly contributed to the fact that many men have been absent from the family due to welfare laws that prevent the unmarried fathers to be present in the household.

For example, children need their father for all kinds of fundamental, emotional reasons_ Boys need rough and tumble play, and a male role model. Girls need fathers toexperience a loving relationship with a man. This is important for girls when they start looking for a mate. Dr. Horn says in the National Fatherhood Initiative, *Missing Fathers Take Big Toll,* "if they have the expectation that a man should be like Dad, they will be more likely to hold out for that positive role model."[29] Once a child has been abused, it causes them to seek acceptance and approval outside of the family environment_ This in turn produces children with bad or imperfect judgment. The black man constantly struggles with those who are in his family and those on the outside. He is determined to provide the same type of lifestyle as the white man. For more than one reason, he finds himself falling short in efforts to obtain a well-rounded life.

When an unmarried black female becomes pregnant, before she can apply for any assistance, she has to make the decision of whether or not to tell the truth regarding the whereabouts of the unborn child's father. The "midnight raids" that were so frequently used against African American women in the 1940s and 1950s and which were declared illegal by the Supreme Court seem to be coming back_ According to the newsletter, *Welfare to Work,* in Hartford, Connecticut, city police are conducting early morning raids on the homes of recipients in a sweep to catch "deadbeat dads." In order for her to obtain any type of government assistance, she has to keep the father out of the picture. These types of actions produce male children that have no father figure in their lives. Once the father's whereabouts are known, regardless of the age, the father is directed to pay child support. It amazes me how a male between the ages of fourteen and sixteen years 'of age can be considered as responsible adults. Most often, the male's parent will step in and assume the responsibility of helping to raise their grandchildren. If a male cannot afford to pay child support, he is then arrested and placed in detention centers and charged with non-support.

---

[29] Wade F. Horn, *National Father Initiative, Missing Fathers Take Big Toll.* Montgomery Advertiser, December 1997.

This action settles nothing because then we have a fatherless child, no male role model, and a mother striving to make it in a world as a single parent. Most people would say that if a boy or young man is having sex, he should be responsible enough to deal with the consequences. This is all true and good, but what type of job can a young uneducated teen obtain in today's society? The cycle for the young black mate continues to the next generation.

Now that we have discussed the monetary and educational factors, there is one more factor left and that is the social stress and how is contributes to this topic. The social environments of the low-income areas or ghetto have very strong effects on the black male whether positive or negative. Every person that grows up in these communities has to make it work for them. They have to create their own world within a world. if you would imagine for a second what goes on when a boy has to walk home from school alone. He is faced with all types of adversities_ He is offered drugs, he is picked on, and he is ridiculed. To deal with this every day, it is a constant conflict with no resolution in sight; however, that same child has to make the decision of whether to be a part of the growing problem or to start a new chapter and do the unheard of He must look toward his own future and do that which is right and make positive choices.

There is always going to be negativity in the world and also in our communities. This is something that we cannot totally eliminate; however, it is something that we as a people can emerge from. We can work harder to instill the right values in our children and we can obtain help from outside organizations, and also after school programs. The struggle for the black man is mostly based on his own outlook and perception of what he thinks his life should be like. His real constant struggle is that he is looking for love and affection. The reason why a large number of children come into conflict with society is because they are unsatisfied. They have an increased thirst for attention and gratification and these same children become adults with the same needs. The young black man who is determined to succeed in life, and who is determined to be that good provider for his family, he needs to be reassured by his community and society that his good works and deeds are being recognized.

Blacks in general have always been labeled as the problem race, the race without a purpose. Therefore, it is easy to believe that everyone else has a lesser opinion of our race. With all of these attributes, it makes life a little bit harder for a black male to stay focused on doing the right thing with so much negativity surrounding him. It is somewhat acceptable for the other races to have their opinion, but when it comes from our own race, it is harder to accept.

The Growing Amount of Young Black Males Incarcerated at Early Ages

Nationwide, African Americans represent 15% of the population, 26% of juvenile arrests, 44% of youth who are detained, 46% of the youth who are judicially waived to criminal court, and 58% of the youth admitted to state prisons. Incarceration rates of African Americans and other minorities are so high that criminal justice has become the civil rights movement of this generation.

African-American Youth at Each

Stage of the Justice System

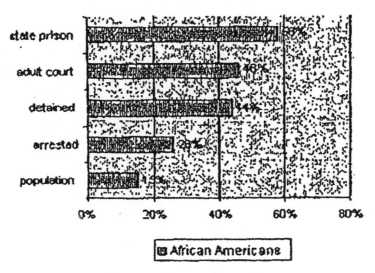

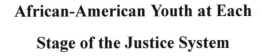

African American youth with felony arrests ace 4.4 times more likely than white youth with felony rates to be sentenced to the California Youth Authority. Hispanic and Asian youth with felony arrests are 3.8 times more likely than white you with felony arrests to be sentenced to the California Youth Authocity.[30]

It should be no surprise that blacks have always been treated as the number one suspect at any age. The police and other law officials focus on the poor black communities, as they know at any given time they are going to see groups of young black males standing on the corners. So why would they go to the white communities when they make guaranteed arrests in our community? They arrest our males for selling drugs on the street, but they seldom go to the suburbs and arrest the drug dealers that sell behind closed doors. The same crimes are being committed by whites, as well as blacks. If there is no difference in the crime, why is there a difference in the time given by a judge?

---

[30] Mark Smoker, *Building Blocks for Youth For a Fair and Effective Youth Justice System.* Youth Law Center, President and Spokesperson. And Justice for Some, 2000.

It is true that we should not stereotype anyone, but tell me the last time you walked past a group of young black males and felt safe. We see it every day, they look like criminals by the way they are dressed and the untidy way they wear their hair. The first thing we say is that he looks bad, or he looks like he will rob me. We are not being fair to the countless youth who are striving to make something of themselves. All we need to do 'is stop looking at them through the eyes of the juvenile detention centers. They all arc not condemned to a life of crime. Most of these first time offenders will never return to the detention centers simply because they have learned their lessons.

If we are to make a difference in the declining number of black arrested, we need to address the unfairness in the criminal laws. We need to train and teach our young people that even though society has given up on the black males and pre-labeled them as a dying and incarcerated generation, we can change our future and their future. We should work harder to educate the ones who are interested in becoming somebody and succeeding in life. We know that once they pass through the juvenile detention centers it could be the beginning of a road going nowhere but downhill. Despite the unbelievable suggestions that black males are confronted with certain hardships, they tend to drop out of school before they have even given it a chance. Once these males decide that an education is non-essential in their lives, they find other avenues to make money and function in society.

Dr. Pedro Nouguera, a professor of education at the University of California, Berkeley states that, "There is no doubt that severe problems exist for many individuals who are both Black and male. However, can we or should we conclude that these problems are primarily caused by or somehow related to the race gender of those individuals who experience them?"[31] This a fair question, when we look at

---

[31]   *tinr, Black Youth: Part 2. In* Motion, page 3.

or examine the number of youths in detention centers, separating them by race and gender. We need to look at the whole picture instead of the smaller view. We need to question the backgrounds of these individuals. We need to seek organizations that can aid them in developing a different mindset. There is no reason why the number of offenders of any race should be growing in leaps and bounds. These are our young people and they are our future.

Instead of spending money on finding ways to building new facilities and increasing the pay of high officials, we need to find ways and programs that would decrease the number of non-violent offenders sentenced to these penile institutions. There must be a better way and a better alternative than the ones currently used. The system must be made to eventually work in our favor for the good of all those involved. We can no longer pais up precious opportunities for establishing laws and rules that work. We are sadly mistaken if we believe that by placing these youths in institutions the problem of juvenile delinquency will just go away. Not so_ Juvenile Delinquency will continue to increase the cost of human and financial responsibilities.

Chapter 3

Concerns About Juveniles Prosecuted
In The Juvenile Justice System

Continuing Educational Programs

The juvenile facilities now offer various educational programs to help give these youngsters some type of trade or decent education. Their needs are determined in terms of academics, vocational training, and personal needs. It should be the goal of every juvenile center to provide appropriate educational services to school age youth residing in the detention center. Criteria for admission to and release from the detention center are based upon the level of progress made by the juveniles, as well as the juvenile court system to a certain degree. The instructional program for each detained child is geared and centered to fit his/her individual needs within the confines of the detention facility.

When a child has been receiving prior special education services in his/her public school, and is admitted with an existing problem, it is the responsibility of the educational personnel at the detention center to ensure the continued special treatment with any modification, as may be necessary, due to the nature of the child's detainment. Children without an individual learning program continue to receive education to meet their individual needs with a curriculum that follows as closely as possible to the student's regular school education program before he/she was detained.

The educational staff assigned to the detention center continues the long practice of working closely with each student's home school in an effort to assure that the individual's educational transition into and out of the detention center setting will be as smooth as possible. This will also assist the child in avoiding any failing grades.

School counseling should be a planned, structural program of services designed to aid children in mastering the academic, personal, social, and career interests which are important to the development of academic, technical, and life skills. The primary task of the school counselor is to assist students and their parents in identifying the appropriate steps that will provide a positive academic, social, and career direction.

Program services would include individual counseling and small group rap sessions, consultation with the significant adults in children lives coordination of the school-wide guidance program, as well as services with community agencies. These program services should be balanced between prevention and intervention and they should be based on the needs of students. Because education is critical to rehabilitation for troubled youth, it is no doubt that it should be considered the strongest function of the detention center. Helping all troubled youth acquire educational skills is also one of the most effective approaches to the prevention of delinquency.

Literacy skills are essential to meet the demands of a complex, world in school and at work. Higher levels of literacy are associated with lower rates of juvenile delinquency and also re-arrests. While illiteracy and poor academic performance are not direct causes of delinquency, they show a strong link between literacy skills and the likelihood of involvement in. the juvenile justice system.

While the majority of detained and committed youth have severe to moderate skill deficits, and prior school experiences marked by truancy, suspension, and expulsion, others may be performing at or above grade level. As a result, juvenile correctional education programs should provide the following comprehensive range of options:

- Literacy and functional skills for students with significant cognitive, behavioral, or learning problems;

- General Educational Development (GED) preparation for students not likely to return to public schools; and desire to finish high school;

- Pre-vocational and vocational education for those students wanting to learn a trade and seek employment upon release; and

- Problems creating academic programs within juvenile corrections are frequently associated both with characteristics of incarcerated youth, and with the operation of the facilities themselves. Youth enter correctional settings with learning disabilities, behavior problems, and substance abuse issues that present difficulties in educational programming. At the same time, juvenile correctional institutions often have limited capacity to support educational interventions for the youth confined to their care and custody. Major problems include overcrowding, isolation of correctional schools from education reform practices and from public schools, and inadequate aftercare services. Special education services in juvenile corrections are started in the larger aspect of academic and vocational programs. Juvenile correctional education programs may fail to educate youth with disabilities when they lack effective processes to screen, evaluate, and identify youth for special education; implement instructional strategies to address teaming or behavioral problems; involve parents, guardians, or surrogates; implement appropriate instructional strategies to address learning or behavioral problems; and organize transition services for youth released to the community.

In addition, accommodations for youth with disabilities are not always implemented in the school. Youth with disabilities who do not receive appropriate special education and related services may be more vulnerable to exclusion from school for alleged disciplinary infractions in the correctional education program and within the larger institution. If these issues are not addressed, so many of our young people will be lost in the system.

It is a true statement that all of our youth are not bad and some of them do not belong in these detention centers. It is evident that we are not at all happy with the way our juvenile justice system is being handled today. As Justice O'Connor urged in a report to the Justice System, "Radically disparate treatment of juveniles within the justice system necessitates that legislators and members of the legal profession make drastic improvements of the juvenile justice system and eliminate racial inequities on a priority basis. We cannot expect that young people who are treated unfairly and disparately solely because of their race of ethnicity will have a respect for the judicial system."[32]

A good number of these young people have medical issues that control their behavior. It is sad that no one will take time to investigate the reason why these children act and behave the way they do. There is a reason for all of their actions. We need to take the time out and question the extent of their problem, instead of just throwing them behind bars and choosing to ignore the need for physiological help. Some may think that the added time spent on diagnosis or providing special services is merely a waste of time for the court systems. Conversely, some of the offenders placed in these facilities may not fare too well. They are considered violent and placed in isolation for their own protection, oftentimes becoming suicidal and depressed. These types of actions do not help the individual. Instead, they tend to show added withdrawal. This will in time hinder their ability to learn and progress. The Juvenile Justice System will be responsible for the care of these individuals, as well as all of the legal aspects regarding their conditions. The wave of school

---

[32]   Statement of Justice O'Connor to The American Bar Association on Perceptions of the U.S. Justice System in 1999, as reported in the Washington Post (May 16, 999).

violence perpetrated by young people has become a household concern across our nation. Experts in the field of child and adolescent mental health are often asked to provide explanations for such behavior; although they have been unable to predict or explain behavior fully. It is nearly impossible for them to attempt to understand and provide solutions to the current epidemic of school violence. It should be understood that the violence among our youth is an expression of anger, which results from feeling alienated and misunderstood.

Adolescents who are disconnected from adults and who have not internalized values and morals often turn to negative "heroes" glorified by the popular culture. These heroes provide answers and allow teens to feel understood and accepted. Many adults tend to minimize teens' passion for dark characters and explain their fascination as "just a stage." The challenge for all adults, including professionals and teachers, should be to convince youth that we are willing to listen and help.

Much of the therapy needed should be focused on educating parents, teachers, and school administrators about effective ways to interact with, and meet the needs of these teens. We all must listen closely to our children, respond quickly when they are troubled, and do our utmost to identify and eliminate the factors that contribute to violence among young people.

Credible Legal Assistance

Some have said that judges on the State and Federal level are known for exercising discretion in their sentencing which tends to favor whites. As a result, many of our black officials continually argue that judicial discretion must be somewhat controlled since those serving as jurors have shown themselves unable to handle the responsibility of sentencing without imparting their own personal beliefs and opinions. These complaints were some of the main reason why people began to believe that sentencing should be placed in the supposedly more able hands of legislators. Unfortunately, those persons never considered that legislators also had similar ideas and would likely construct laws which reflected their opinions about others. Since some judges were making federal sentencing a mockery, the debate seemed to focus on the practices of federal judges. The legislators took it upon themselves to try and eliminate race from sentencing by making it uniform according to the offense. They argued that no matter who committed the crime, they should all be punished exactly the same. They even limited the sentencing discussion to the offender's criminal history and the offense he was convicted of. For some reason, these lawmakers never considered that people of certain economic backgrounds are convicted of different crimes because of their access and means to commit certain crimes. They seemed to take a blind attitude toward who would be disproportionately affected by their new laws. They felt that since crack was the new culprit of America, it should have a higher and more severe penalty than cocaine, despite the fact that both are the same drug_ They increased the penalties concerning crack and watched as large number of prisoners were arrested at three to five times their prior rate.

Undoubtedly, these politicians and officials felt they had created a uniform standard for all crimes so race would not be a factor judges could consider. Because of their inherent biases against minorities, most politicians never—even considered that their laws would greatly affect the black communities. These lawmakers may have just been guilty of benign neglect toward the types of offenses minorities are convicted of and thought they were making laws that would decrease the incarceration rate of minorities. I hope these lawmakers did not set out to create laws that would increase minority incarceration, while allowing white rates to remain stable or decrease.

The system has allowed this type of process to move completely into the hands of the police and prosecutors. If the prosecutor refuses to file a downward departure motion for the, defendant due to his help as an informant or because he feels as though that individual deserves a break,—the courts have shown it is not willing to declare a sentence below the mandated sentence. While the few brave district court judges should be commended, there are no indications to suggest their efforts will accomplish anything but allowing the offender a few extra months with his family members before the appellate court reinstates his original sentence.

Failure to Separate Children from Adults

The lack of suitable juvenile detention facilities in this country is discussed often and is currently part of a study by county government Someday, issues such as these will be settled and not just discussed over a cup of coffee. A juvenile offender who is accused of a criminal offense and taken into custody is placed in a holding facility, where there are also convicted adults. Now, often the system will do that which is right, but every once and a while someone slips through the cracks of our legal system.

Unfortunately, some of these juveniles are not separated from the convicted adults. For that child who is not securely detained away from the adults, he is put in harm's way and subject to negative conflict.

Many of Maryland's jails do not separate children from adult inmates. In Frederick and Washington Counties, for example, jail staff stated that children are routinely commingled with adults. Even in the largest facilities, they found that children are exposed to adult inmates to a degree that would not meet the "sight and sound" separation standard that would be required if these children were charged in the juvenile courts. Juveniles may be housed with adults even in the largest facilities?[33]

We have to consider the fact that children who get arrested are afraid and very unsure of where they are headed in the system. Sure, we have those who put on a tough show, but these are still frightened children no matter what crimes they have committed. When that door closes and they can no longer see their parents, they become fearful of their surroundings, and to make it worse, they are placed in facilities with adults. Some of these adults are longtime convicts with nothing to lose. As a result, we are taking these children and placing them in the hands of danger. We are allowing inmates to have their way with them, and we are allowing inmates to further corrupt them. Separation is a very needed task. We must do everything in our power to at least change the way these juveniles are handled by the legal system. A juvenile that is currently serving time wrote the following words:

> "Being here with adults, that ain't going to rehabilitate me, its just teaching me to be a better criminal. They looking to lock me up, throw away the key, leave me with no hope. [need to break out the cycle, get me some services and treatment so I can be a productive member of society. Being an adult, that's right around the corner. I be asking for treatment, but I'm seventeen, six foot three, 200 pounds. I still got the mind of a minor, but they look at my body first."[34]

---

[33] *Human Rights Watch Interview with LaMont Flanagan,* Commissioner, Division of Pretrial Detention and Services, Maryland Department of Public Safety and Correctional Services, Baltimore, Maryland 5/ 1 1 /99.

[34] James S_ (not his actual name), *Interview in the Montgomery County Detention Center,* July 30, 1999.

How much more evidence do we need to see that the current plan is not working the way in which it was designed? We have to stop accepting whatever is handed down to us. This is why it is so important to vote and participate in the decisions that are made by government, especially those decisions that directly affect our loved ones. Many believe that it is time to treat juvenile offenders like adults by subjecting them to adult justice. At present, we send only a few juveniles to adult/courts. Most of those charged, even repeat offenders, end up in more lenient juvenile courts

I am in no way condoning the actions of our juveniles, but I am stating that we need to change the guidelines that have been set in motion for our youthful offenders. What reason would we have to place youths with adults? There are gangs in jail, drug dealers; everything that is out here on the street is in jail. How are we ever going to rehabilitate the young people and give them positive guidance if we put them in places that have the same practices and crimes found on the street? Mark Soler cites in remarks before the Senate Youth Violence Subcommittee that "the most disturbing aspect of the new bill regarding juvenile justice is the well-founded fear that the thousands of young people slated to be placed in adult prisons and jails are more likely to be raped, assaulted, and commit suicide. Surveys have documented the higher risk juveniles face when placed in adult institutions, and people who work with youth know all-too-familiar stories. In Ohio, a 15-year old girl is sexually assaulted by a deputy jailer after she is placed in an adult jail for a minor infraction. In Kentucky, 30 minutes after a 15-year old is put in a jail cell following an argument with his mother, the youth hangs himself.[35]

There is a large number of troubled youth in our society, and some of them are not as violent as others. Many of these individuals were arrested for committing

---

[35] Mark I. Soler, Remarks before the Senate Youth Violence Subcommittee_ Senate Judiciary Committee, on the core requirements of the Juvenile Justice Act and the Violent Juvenile and Repeat Offender Act of 1997, Washington, D_C.

minor crimes. With this being the case, it serves no positive purpose in putting them behind bars with adults. There are two systems: one for adults and one for children_ We should strive to keep the two systems as far apart from each other as possible. I realize that we have those young individuals who have committed crimes some adults would not think of doing, and if they are 18 years or older, then yes they should be placed in adult detention centers. When I speak of juveniles, please know that I am referring to those persons under the age of 18.

Some juvenile-related expenditure is funded by local governments or from other sources. The funding from local governments or other sources is not included in the expenditures in this report. Examples include the following:

- Juvenile bureaus in Oklahoma, Tulsa, and Comanche counties provide services that are similar to services provided by the Office of Juvenile Affairs in all other counties. County government resources primarily fund the three bureaus.

- The Office of Juvenile Affairs contracts with various youth service agencies to provide various services. Those agencies also receive support from other state agencies and various other local sources_

- Some of the federal grants administered and awarded by the Office of Juvenile Affairs require the recipient to provide matching funds from local resources for those grants.

Youthful Offenders

Since implementation of the Youthful Offender Act in 1998, 371 juveniles have been convicted as Youthful Offenders. During FY 2001, 117 juveniles were convicted as Youthful Offenders including 4 sentenced as adults and transferred to the custody or supervision of the Department of Correction, 100 remanded to the custody of OJA and 13 remanded to OJA supervision. Five Youthful Offenders originally remanded to the custody or supervision of OJA during FY 2001 were later bridged to the Department of Corrections. As of the end of the fiscal year, the Office of Juvenile Affairs had responsibility for 212 Youthful Offenders including 20 under supervision and 192 in custody.

Literacy Assessments

All juveniles adjudicated by a district court as Delinquent or as In Need of Supervision are required to receive a test, such as the Slosson Oral Reading Test (Revised), to determine their reading level if they are under the supervision of OJA. Five hundred and sixty-nine juveniles received this test during fiscal year 2001, 29.7% (169) scored below grade level and were required to participate in a literacy skills improvement program. The results of the test per age group is provided below:

Age Group	Total Juveniles Tested	Number and Percent Scoring Below Grade level and Requiring Improvement
Under 13	28	14 (50.0%)
13 and 14 year olds	105	22 (20.9%)
15 and 16 year olds	224	75 (33.4%)
17 and older	212	58 (27.3%)

Every year, there are more and more juveniles incarcerated with adults, and they become lost in the system if they do not have loved ones that push the issue of separation. A good way to remedy this would be to set up an evaluation program for the juvenile facilities, so that a better track record is kept on the number of juveniles processed into these facilities. We can never be allowed to sit back and assume that this system in working correctly. We must be willing to take matters into our own hands. 1410 minor should be lost in the system, especially when they are finally found in adult detention centers, and the damage has already been done to their minds, as well as their physical bodies.

Chapter 4

The Preparations That Are Made or Not Made
To Return Juveniles Back Into Society

Positive Youth Development

What Is Positive Youth Development? Positive Youth Development is a policy perspective that emphasizes providing services and opportunities to support all young people in developing a sense of competence, usefulness, belonging, and empowerment. While individual programs can provide youth development, activities or services, the youth development approach works best when entire communities, including young people, are involved in creating a continuum of services and opportunities that youth need to grow into happy and healthy adults. The fully developed and diversified after care program is far from the norm in most communities. Such a plan is often no more than an idea in the minds of some corrections experts. The resources needed to implement a comprehensive help program for returnees already exist in many local communities. However, cooperation, coordination, and planning are still needed to bring all of the necessary elements together.

Simply put, youth development is a life process that everyone goes through. The goal of the positive youth development approach is to ensure that all adolescents experience this life stage positively.

Why Should I Care About Positive Youth Development? The catchy answer is that young people are this nation's most valuable resource. The reality is that youth have talents and needs that communities can no longer afford to ignore. When we fail to provide youth with support and opportunities, as adults they may experience unemployment, have drug or alcohol problems, commit crimes, and become a drain on community resources. When young people are nurtured by caring adults, given opportunities to become involved in education or work that builds their skills, and are supported and protected during challenging times, and are actively engaged in community activities, they become valuable contributors to the quality of community life. Engaging youth in communities simply makes sense, both fiscally and ethically.

Central to the positive youth development approach is an understanding that all youth need access to developmental opportunities. They, of course, also need reliable information about behaviors that put them at risk, and at some point during adolescence, they may need prevention and intervention services. These services are far more effective when they are part of a community-designed system of support and developmental opportunities that provide young people with chances to try new ventures or work toward dreams they had not thought attainable. As young people gain confidence and skills, they shift their decision-making outlook from the short term to the long term, making choices that preserve their dreams and goals and help them avoid behaviors that put them at risk. The positive youth development approach emphasizes fully preparing young people to succeed and contribute now and as adults, rather than focusing simply on ensuring that young people are not engaged in risky behaviors. Nonetheless, risk reduction and problem avoidance are often outcomes of developmentally focused programs.

Many local programs offer young people both developmental opportunities and prevention and intervention services. The Boys & Girls Clubs of America, National 4-R Council, and YMCA of the USA, for example, are national organizations that promote the positive youth development approach through their local program affiliates. These programs provide young people with the access to developmental services and activities and construct positive connections between youth and other young people and adults_ They also offer young people valuable information and learning experiences that help them choose healthy lifestyles_ Many local programs offer young people both developmental opportunities and prevention and intervention services.

Viable and Suitable Work Programs

When juveniles who are of workable age return to the community and society, they must be equipped to handle themselves as responsible adults. In order to gain this new outlook, it is important that they receive the adequate amount of help before returning to society. The detention center can play an important role by providing a suitable work-study environment to these individuals while incarcerated_

Work Project: A specific task that a youth can work on in a secured or non-secured setting to make court ordered restitution or community service. Work projects emphasize individual accountability through vigorous physical work to accomplish goals significant to the community and help youth develop a sense of accomplishment based on their own positive efforts. The physical labor involves such things as ground keeper, shoveling snow, and trail building in state and federal parks, as well as graffiti removal. Points from these activities are used to pay off court-ordered restitution or community service obligations. Typically; this work benefits the community at large, nonprofit organizations, and special groups such as the elderly or the disabled. Work camps and work programs have become an important part of the services offered by the Division of Youth Corrections.

1. Youth age 14 to 18. Youth who have been judged as delinquent by the courts and have failed to abide by conditions of probation or failed other community based programs, should be recommended to attend these special work camps or boot camps.

2. Youth placed at these facilities have been convicted of such crimes as auto theft, home burglary, assault, sale and use of drugs, armed robbery, and aggravated burglary.

3. Youth must be physically able to perform manual labor, should not have any injuries, disabilities, etc., which would interfere with work assignments. A physical examination should be completed within the previous six months to insure the youth can handle the required physical demands of the program_

4. Violent youth (youth physically assaulting residents and/or staff) should not be referred. If placed in these environments we are placing others at risk_

5. Youth with emotional or psychological problems should not be referred. The attention that they require cannot be rendered in camps. Youth on psychotropic medication or other medication for depression or other psychological problems should not be referred or ordered. The medical program at these camps and centers is not equipped to service these youth_

6. Youth should not be a suicide risk. Any prior attempts at suicide or hurting self are high indicators the youth may be at risk.

Youth should be required to shave and have hair no longer than above the ears, not over their collars. Youth should not be permitted to have braids or twist. All youth should wear a uniform. No foul language should be permitted. No gang or street talk should ever be allowed or tolerated. These are the things that they are accustomed to on the street. If we are to help them, then we need to eliminate those things that they are most comfortable in doing.

In addition, the detention center or work camps should be prepared to offer a variety of other programs including, behavioral modification, family conferences, school conferences, social skills and life skills classes, as well as conflict resolutions. All are important in returning these individuals to society and to their communities.

Juveniles also participate in various community service projects including basic maintenance and beautification assignments, as well as social service projects that serve needy populations, the same populations that they have committed crimes against.

During the middle part of the program, each juvenile identifies a project that will benefit his or her community. The juvenile must complete the project in order to advance to the final month of the program. Before juveniles complete the program, they should be assigned a mentor. Mentors meet with program staff, probation staff, and guardians at least three times while the juvenile is in the program. The goal for young people must go beyond survival to development and involvement. It is in their and our interest to ensure an acceptable standard of living and protect them from economic, sexual, emotional, and physical harm, but their productivity and security will depend on developing their full potential and engaging them not only as beneficiaries, but as participants and problem-solvers. This program should be set up as a one-day workshop that is based upon an educational evaluation incorporating group discussions, instructor facilitation, and reasoning and decision-making skills. In addition, participants view taped presentations and perform simple exercises using a basic workbook that they are free to keep after the program is over.

While the juveniles are engaged in the group's discussions and skill training sessions, their parents will be expected to meet separately to discuss what may have led their son or daughter to participate in the unlawful activity and what they can do to make their living environment better when their child has completed the program. After the program is completed, the parents and the juveniles will have a better understanding of what causes minors to commit juvenile crimes and the importance of good citizenship on a personal and community level. Prayerfully, this will eliminate the repeat offenders, and these individual will be able to take what they have learned back into their communities and schools and apply them to their everyday life.

Support Groups for Juveniles

The young crime victims are offered counseling and the opportunity to participate in mediation. They also receive support from volunteer law students who accompany the 'victim and his or her family through the judicial process from the initial police report to the completion of proceedings. The support center also provides an open telephone line to which crime victims and their families can turn for advice, support and practical assistance. All assistance is provided free of charge and those turning to the support center are entitled to complete anonymity.

The way that young victims react to the crimes they have experienced varies considerably. Without exception, the victims that have been in contact with the support center have experienced psychological problems as a result of the indignities that the crime has involved. Besides being subjected to the crime itself, additional psychological injuries may be sustained as a result of the failure of adult witnesses to intervene. The police investigation is discontinued as a result of the fact that the police are not always able to find the perpetrators, the provision of little or no support during stressful court proceedings or the possible release of the perpetrator. Further indignity may be experienced if the victim does not then receive a damage award from an insurance company. The function of the support center involves working through and alleviating the consequences of these injuries. Among the principle objectives of the support center is to make special resources available for the work conducted with young crime victims, and thus to take their experiences of crime seriously, so that they do not lose faith in either the community of which they are a part, the adult world, or the justice system.

Chapter 5

The Discrimination Concerning Black Juveniles
and White Juveniles

Legal Representation

With so many cases going through our courts, there are always a significant number of cases that involve questionable issues of fact that can only be resolved by a judge or jury. In each of the cases it handles, the Public Defenders' Office works to protect the rights of the accused to be treated with dignity, fairness, and due, process within our legal system. The right of one charged with a crime to counsel may not be considered fundamental and essential to fair trials in some countries, but it is in ours. From the very beginning, our state laws have put great emphasis on procedural safeguards designed to assure fair trials before impartial court officials in which every defendant stands equal before the law.

In *Justice on Trial,* the Civil Rights Leadership Conference reported that black adult and juvenile makes are over-represented in the criminal justice system, and that black women are imprisoned at a rate seven times greater than white women. The report indicates "there has been an increase in their incarceration rate in excess of 400% in recent years. Further, three-fourths of the women according to the report were mothers, and two-thirds have children under 18."[36]

As a sensible matter, however, there is very little disagreement over the facts in most criminal cases. Our county's well-trained law enforcement officers and

---

[36] *Justice on Trial,* Chapter VT, p.3. Amnesty International, Report 2000 issued recently to President Clinton includes the inquiry into complaints of widespread sexual abuse of inmates at the Cluvanna Correctional Center. 2000_

experienced prosecutors do an outstanding job of filtering out most unsustainable criminal charges before they ever get to court. As a result, the large majority of cases are resolved by negotiated discussions without a trial, and the most important aspect of a defendant's case is likely to be the pronouncement of sentence. However, the role of defense counsel during the sentencing stage of a criminal case is highly important and cannot be overstated.

The Public Defender's Office has been an active partner in adult and juvenile drug court programs, as well as court-supervised programs centered at preventing violence through anger management. Their purpose is to protect the innocent from wrongful conviction, but the great majority of their work consists of counseling and persuading their clients to take advantage of the host of rehabilitative services offered in the community and by the courts, and to use those services to produce positive change in their lives. We know that positive change leads to the kind of personal transformation that in many ways decrease the likelihood that the clients will become repeat offenders and face an ever escalating series of criminal actions.

Another responsibility or service of the Public Defender's caseload consists of people facing the possibility of the permanent loss of custody of their children due to allegations of abuse or, more typically, neglect which causes juvenile delinquency_ If any of the allegations are found to be true, parents are put under social worker supervision and placed in programs geared to improving their parenting skills and resolving issues such as drug addiction that tend to interfere with the ability to be effective parents. In this area of law, particularly the stewardship of an experienced Public Defender lawyer can often be the difference between family reunion and the permanent loss of parental rights. No less than criminal defendants facing jail or prison for criminal behavior, people suffering from mental illness are likewise entitled to the assistance of counsel when the government seeks to deprive them of their personal liberty.

One of the most serious problems is the fact that some probation officers consistently portray black youth differently than white youth in their written court reports. They tend to attribute blacks' delinquency to negative personality traits. These assessments and reports have a profound effect because the written probation reports often determine what sentence may be recommended. According to the survey produced and reported by the Leadership Conference on Civil Rights entitled, "How the Public Views State Courts," "unequal treatment of minorities characterizes every stage of the process. Black and Hispanic Americans, and other minority groups as well, are victimized by disproportionate targeting and unfair treatment by police and other frontline law enforcement officials; by racially skewed charging and plea bargaining decisions of prosecutors; by discriminatory sentencing practices; and by failure of judges, elected officials, probation officers, and other criminal justice policy makers to redress the inequities that become more glaring every day." [37]

After probation, once inside the courtroom, a juvenile will be treated fairly, said several attorneys and youth who have been through the system. But Eric Dorsch, a Legal Aid attorney who has worked in the Bronx and Brooklyn for four years said, "Certain judges are biased." Of the thousands of cases he has worked on, Dorsch said he has seen several instances of a juveniles "getting harsher punishment because of the color of their skin."

Racial Profiling

In his report, *Building Block For A Fair and Effective Youth Justice System,* Mark Smoler says, "We are taking our minority children and youth and putting them in the worse location. It reverses a long trend in American policy not to have

---

[37] Survey, entitled *"How the Public Views State Courts,"* conducted by the National Center for State • -Summary, p.2. t999.

children imprisoned with hardened adult criminals. Researchers used data from state and federal arrest records, juvenile court actions, detention, and waivers to adult court and incarceration. They found, for example, that black youth are 15% of the population under 18, but comprise one-third of youth referred to, formally processed by and convicted in juvenile court. Blacks also account for 40 percent of the youth sent to adult courts and 58 percent of the youth sent to adult prison, said the report entitled, "And Justice for Sorne."[38] The Urban League and other civil rights groups joined in its release. The number of Latino youth may be understated because most state court and prison records designate them as white. With this type of practice, how do we ever determine an accurate number when race is involved or questioned?

The groups that compiled this report, nonetheless, praised the comprehensive report, which followed several recent juvenile justice studies, as hard evidence of something they have long suspected: minority youth are victims of racial bias built into the justice system. Even when types of crime were considered, minorities were more likely to go to jail or prison. Among youth with no prior record arrested for violent crimes, including murder, rape and robbery, a large number of blacks were incarcerated, compared to a lesser amount of youth of other races.

According to a written statement submitted by Human Rights Watch to the Secretary General, "for drug offenses, which can carry a wide range of penalties, the numbers of black youth are convicted on a larger scale as compared to whites. Although the prevalence of both crack and powder cocaine use is higher among Whites than African Americans (more than half of all crack cocaine users are White), 96% of those prosecuted for crack possession and facing the higher crack sentences are Black or Latino. Higher arrest and prosecution rates for African American drug offenders and the long mandatory prison sentences imposed for crack cocaine

---

[38] Mark Smoter. *Budding Blocks for Youth For A Fair and Effective Youth Justice System.* Youth Law Center, President and spokesperson. 2000.

offenses in contrast to powder cocaine are a principal reason that Blacks account for 60% of the federal prison population."[39]

Racial, ethnic, and related identities can be a powerful source of cohesion, values, and identity that strengthen and enrich individual and community lives. These identities can also be manipulated for political gain, employed to oppress and destroy, and used as criteria for determining whose rights are respected and whose are obliterated. Although the international community cannot remove all race and descent-based doctrines from political discourse, it can and must work to ensure that the power of the state does not promote race or descent-based hatred and is not employed to perpetuate and deepen race or descent-based distinctions in the exercise of basic rights.

Discrimination in the administration of justice, whether in policing, criminal prosecutions, trials, sentencing, or imprisonment can cause extraordinary harm to individuals and society alike, and have lasting consequences for future generations. Members of racial, ethnic, and other minorities or vulnerable groups often face harassment, arbitrary detention, and abusive treatment by the taw enforcement apparatus and disparate treatment by prosecutors and the courts.

Police disproportionately target members of marginalized groups for arrest in many countries. Members of these groups may also face disproportionate prosecutions, unfair trials, and disproportionately severe sentences on criminal charges. Humiliating treatment, beatings, sexual abuse, and shooting deaths of members of marginalized groups often contrast with treatment extended to others and members of these groups, who have little recourse to legal remedies to abuse.

---

[39]   Racism, Racial Discrimination, Xenophobia and All Forms of Discrimination; written statement submitted by Human Rights Watch, a non-governmental organization in special consultative status_ 1999_

These trends were true in all offense categories and were especially notable among drug offenses (Table 5). In 1997, 59% of adjudicated drug offense cases involved a white youth, while white youths accounted for 45% of drug offense cases resulting in out-of-home placement and 64% of cases resulting in formal probation. In contrast, 39% of drug offense cases involved an African American youth, while African American youths accounted for 53% of adjudicated drug offense cases resulting in out-of-home placement and 34% of drug offense cases receiving formal probation.[40]

Table 5: Adjudicating Cases Resulting in Residential Placement and Probation, 1997			
	Percent of Cases		
	Adjudicated Delinquent	Placed on Probation	Residential Placement
Person			
White	58%	59%	56%
African American	39%	37	41
Other	4	3	4
Total	100%	100%	100%
Property			
White	69%	70%	65%
African American	27	26	31
Other	4	4	4
Total	100%	100%	100%
Drug	· =		
White	59%	64%	45%
African American	39	34	53
Other	2	2	2
Total	100%	100%	100%
Public Order			
White	64%	64%	62%
African American	33	33	35

---

[40] Source: *Easy Access to Juvenile Court Statistics: 1988-1997* (data presentation and analysis package Office of Juvenile Justice and Delinquency Prevention (1999).

Other	3	3	3
Total	100%	100%	100%
Note: Details may not add to totals due to rounding			

Neutral laws can have great impact on vulnerable minorities or even majorities as a consequence of prosecutorial discretion or sentencing policies or the nature of the law itself. The resulting impact on particular descent-based groups may be vastly disproportionate to the actual involvement of members of these groups in the overall pattern of criminal activity. Criminal penalties that are accompanied by temporary or permanent disenfranchisement further exclude members of groups already facing discriminatory treatment from participation in political life and accentuate their economic, social, and political rnarginalization.

Discriminatory effect can be particularly devastating in the application of the basis for discrimination other than the underlying crime for which the penalty is ostensibly applied routinely enters into the determination of which persons are executed and which persons are allowed to live. The inherent fallibility of all criminal justice systems assures that even when full due process of law as is respected innocent persons are sometimes executed_ Because an execution is irreversible, such miscarriages of justice can never be corrected_

Those facing discrimination can also be denied equal protection by police and the courts when they stand up for their rights in disputes with other private citizens. Police may stand by as attacks are made upon members of a marginalized group or deliberately delay their intervention. Criminal investigations into such crimes, if initiated, may be halfhearted. Police in many countries refuse even to register the complaints of members of marginalized groups distinguished by their race, ethnicity, or descent, while giving special treatment to those attacking them. Members of marginalized groups who are accused of crimes or subjected to generalized suspicion and intimidation are too often also treated with extreme brutality by law enforcement personnel. And police all too often acquiesce in racial attacks by others participating directly in or condoning violent efforts to punish, repress, or banish members of racial minorities who have incurred the wrath of those in power.

Discrimination in criminal justice and other areas of public policy is perhaps most pervasive and deep rooted when the heritage of slavery and legislative segregation remains a potent factor. This sometimes embraces hidden forms of racism that permeate public and private practice across whole societies and finds its clearest expression in the state's administration of justice. Society must be educated in knowing that when comparing criminal process, the juvenile trial system may be somewhat prejudicial. Martin Guggenheim cited that:

"Where judges sit as the sole triers of fact, prejudice is assured. Not only are judges prejudiced in favor of their own system, but frequently the system itself prejudices juveniles who come before them. It is not uncommon for judges to hear more than one case involving the same child over. a period of time. After the first case, the judge learns about the child, his family and environment. As "jurors," judges are extremely cynical. With their knowledge of the common alibis which children use, they would be disqualified automatically if they were on a jury panel. But when a child, perhaps art innocent one, comes before the judge and pleads the same defense the judge disbelieves in another case involving another juvenile a week before, the child will surely loose."[41]

---

[41]   Martin Guggenheim. *Paternalism, Prevention, and Punishment: Pretrial Detention of luveniles.* New York University Law Review, 52:1064-1092_

At the national or local level, discrimination can arise from practices with racist intent, such as racial profiling, in which an individual's presumed race is the determining factor in placing them under suspicion. The mechanisms of criminal justice can equally result in unjustified discriminatory effect where there is no clear racist intent. Discriminatory impact can be shown in patterns of police abuse, arbitrary arrest, incarceration, prosecution, and sentencing. According to an article reported in the New York Times in December 1999, New York Attorney General Eliot Spitzer released the results of an investigation by his office of the "stop and frisk" practices in New York City. It showed that Blacks and Latinos were much more likely to be stopped and searched even when the statistics were adjusted to reflect differing Criminal participation rates in some neighborhoods.[42] Discrimination in a criminal justice system may be deliberate, reflecting invidious bias, or it may flow from ostensibly neutral decisions that nonetheless produce an unjustified racially disparate impact. Some minority officers may be just as harsh on blacks and other minorities. They may feel pressure from peers and supervisors to treat black and Hispanic suspects as tough, if not tougher, than white offenders if they choose to assimilate into the department and be accepted within the police organization. Racial profiling is a fact of life in America and must be addressed. We have all seen the stories about how blacks often have difficulties hailing a taxi cab, renting apartments, getting loans, buying cars, etc. Yet for some unknown reason, we expect the police to perform their duties within the limits of the law unfettered by the cultural and political biases within which they exist. Ultimately, the issue comes down to how we want the police to do their job. If we support proactive policing, then racial profiling will continue to exist. Reactive policing may be the

---

[42] Kevin Flynn, *State Cites Racial Inequality in New York Police Searches.* New York Times. December 1999, at 22.

only solution which says a lot for our law enforcement. In this day and time, we should not have to make decisions such as these.

Clean and Safe Environments

Although we hear many horror stories regarding the condition of juvenile detention centers, there is a surprising fact in today's centers. There is routine health screening that is performed by staff and other outside professionals. The purpose of these screenings is to evaluate and identify those individuals entering into the system with certain medical issues that need constant assistance. With the adequate amount of health supervision, the detention center can help and treat medical problems as well as addictions.

It is not an understatement to say that juvenile facilities are very dangerous places and this contributes mainly to the fact that they are seriously overcrowded. This is one of the reasons why the youth cannot obtain adequate medical and also mental health services, as well as the proper amount of education and recreation. This situation is constantly escalating throughout the juvenile detention centers. The most threatened situation, however, is the amount of tension felt in these centers. Most of the docile youth find themselves fighting to protect themselves against the more violent offenders. These offenders are in need of special attention from the staff regarding suicidal actions and behavior. This special attention includes setting up special suicide prevention programs.

These facilities and institutions are also responsible for maintaining a safe and healthy environment for the offenders, as well as the staff.

Slap on the Wrist

The worse thing that we can do to hurt these juveniles is to make them believe for one minute that the crimes that they are convicted are not serious enough for them to receive punishment. Too many times our young people are let off with just warning& While warnings are okay in their correct place, the violent offenders should be prosecuted to the Midst extent of the law_ This is not to say that they should be mistreated or placed in facilities with adult offenders. However, it says that they should realize that no crime should be or will not be tolerated.

When crimes are committed by our youth, they should be made to pay restitution to the victims affected. They have to learn that just as they have caused heartache for someone's family, the justice system has the ability to cause the same for them. When our children are adolescents, we make allowances for the misbehavior and tend to give no attention to what they do or say to outsiders. We feel as though this is something they will outgrow. Even in the household, we see siblings fighting and disrespecting each other and we overlook it. Mistakenly, we feel there is riot need to worry, however when as they mature, this pattern is passed on into adulthood. At this stage, it becomes harder for the parents to control them, because they have not made it a practice to teach self-respect, which is needed to survive in life. We must start out raising and teaching our children the correct way, and then when they are older they will do the right things and make the right choices.

Anytime a juvenile who appears in the court system time and time again for the same or similar related crimes, the law should be that the punishment is increased. They need to know that the next time they appear before a judge, the likelihood that they will go home with a slap on the wrist will be reduced. The only way that we will ever move forward and save these children, is to show them through tough love that they must be made to obey the laws that have been set to govern them.

Parents are the worse enablers. They know that their children are committing illegal activities and they constantly cloak for them.

If the parents were like they were in the past, they would correct you and then make you apologize to the person whom you committed, a crime against or the person that you offended. The parents need to know that turning a deaf ear to the truth is not helping their children, but is allowing them to go a step further each and every time they break the law. We as parents need to admit to ourselves that we have troubled children and the best way to help them is to obtain the correct professional—help. There are all types of agencies available to our young people; however, it is up to us as individuals to make these systems work on our behalf. After all, they were designed and implemented to aid our children. Programs cannot and will not work unless they have participation. We can no longer afford to see our tax dollars spent on creating these programs, and allow them to sit idle and not be productive on our behalf. There is more help available in this day and age than there ever has been, yet we do not take advantage of the help offered to our young people. Instead, we choose to panic when they come home in trouble.

The parents also need to know that instead of ignoring certain issues, they can help their children by way of demonstrating their faith in their religious beliefs. It is the parents' responsibility to help their children discover religion as something that is an essential part of their lives_ The manner of expressing family religion is not only in what the family lives for, but also in the quality of relationships maintained between family members_ The key is that the positive characteristics will not allow the negative characteristics of delinquency to develop in their children.

Once we admit to ourselves that juvenile delinquency is a serious matter, and that it invades our lives and cause nothing but uncertainty and confusion for all family members, we will be more than ready to find a successful solution. We all know that we live in a changing world, but we must be ready, willing and able to prevent this problem from overtaking our families.

Churches can also participate in helping to set our children in the right direction: It is so important that they be willing to give more attention to the problems. No one and certainly no church can do everything that is required to be done for the youth's sake, but they should seek to do the most needful things and do them from the heart. The most important thing to give a youth is spiritual guidance. They need a sense of values and assurance that life makes sense. Some of these children feel as though they have make wrong choices all of their lives, and when we slap them on the wrist and tell them not to do it again, we are not helping them, we are not giving them what they so desperately are searching for.

We have to stop making life so comfortable for our young people. Half of the young people today do not know the importance of their freedom and the price that was paid to obtain it. We are so quick to say that, "We do not want our kids to grow up hard," because that is what we had to do all of our lives. Well guess what, all we are doing is fooling them into thinking that life owes them something.

Life is only what you make it, your choices have to be positive, and you have to have a determined mind. Youth today do not understand the meaning of earning wages or working hard to get what they want, all they know is give it to me. The system if full of misled young people who thought that they had found an easier way. They thought that their parents did not understand their plight and that they were old fashioned and did not understand the ways of the world. It is a sad fact that our youth have been fooled for so long, and it is partially our own fault because we have created certain situations.

We can no longer be the guilty party in our children's lives. We must lead and direct them to the truth and the reality that they have to be accountable for their actions.

Chapter 6

Avenues to Remedy This Growing Concern
Of Black Youth in the American Justice System

The Court System, State and Local Government

When a juvenile is presented before the court system, the first action that is taken during the court process is to determine whether or not the individual's case should be processed in the criminal justice system rather than in juvenile court. This decision is sometimes based on the nature of the crime. Sometimes what they call a judicial waiver is given by the judge. This waives the juvenile's right to be tried in juvenile court, and instead he is sent to criminal court. In some states, a combination of the youth's age, offense, and prior record places certain juvenile offenders under the jurisdiction of both the juvenile and criminal court. When this happens, the prosecutor is the authority to decide which court will handle the case.

I have found in doing this research along with seeing firsthand that the juvenile laws are slightly worded and hardly applied. It permits extensive abuses in the handling of children by socially controlled agencies whose discretion in greatly unchecked. Instead of protecting children from injustices and uninvited state intervention, the opposite effect often occurs.

African American youth are more likely to be detained by police, but also they are more likely to receive the most severe court dispositions. It is sad that the race and class has influenced the decision making process, with minority and lower class youth receiving the greater dispositions than the white delinquents. To think that our court system has gone to this level is very scary for poor black youth. It is time that we seek to find out just what laws protect our youth. If we have no one in the political office to check and make sure these laws are carried out the way they were intended, then this puts all of us in a bad situation. We are so open-minded to believe that the system is in place to work for our youth that we do not feel the need to take matters into our own hands and make sure that they are operating on a legitimate level. I saw firsthand when I was employed by the Charles Hickey School, which is a juvenile detention center, how the staff treated the inmates. [saw firsthand that some of the juveniles had mental issues and they were kept on medication. Sometimes these facilities will keep the offenders doped up in order to not deal with them or give them the attention that they long to have. I am not sure whether the hiring officials were aware of the inexperience of the staff. It is hard to determine the truth. These are the issues that we need to stay focused on, especially when it involves our family members.

"Black youths are six times more likely to be incarcerated than Whites, even when they are charged with the same crimes and have never been in detention before. Those charged with drug offenses are 48 times more likely than whites to be sentenced to juvenile institutions. On average, when they are prosecuted as adults and sent to prison, they stay 61 days longer than whites convicted of the same crime,—as reported by Candy Hatcher in the *Seattle Post-Intelligencer Reporter* in April, 2000_ [43]

Preventing Teen/Juvenile Pregnancies

Women have tended to become pregnant during their teens and early twenties_ Teenage parenthood is by no means a new social problem, but today, teenage pregnancy in the United States is one of the most serious problems within the

---

[43] Candy Hatcher, *And Justice For Some.* Seattle Post-latelligencer, April 2000.

family. The number of teenage pregnancies has been increasing continuously, even though many ways to prevent this problem have been generated. If this problem is not controlled and solved seriously, it will possibly increase the number of criminals from uneducated persons reared by teenage mothers and affect our society in general.

The increase is of particular concern because teen mothers and their babies face increased risk to their health because they cannot take good care of themselves or their babies; teenage pregnancy probably affects health risks to either a teenage mother or a baby_ Usually, teenagers have poor eating habits, smoke, drink alcohol and take drugs, which increase the risk that their babies will be born with health problems. Furthermore, teenagers are likely to be affected by sexually transmitted diseases, such as Chlarnydia (which can cause sterility), Syphilis (which can cause blindness and death, and death to the infant), and AIDS, which is fatal to the mother and can infect the infant. Also, it is a fact that a baby born to a teenage mother is more at risk than a baby born to an older mother. The studies of The March of Dimes Birth Defects Foundation show that nine percent of teenage girls have low birth weight babies (under 5.5 lbs.), compared to 7 percent of all mothers nationally. Low birth weight babies may have organs that are not fully developed and are 40 times more likely to die in their first month of life than normal weight babies_

Moreover, we must be concerned about the consequences of teenage pregnancy. For example, because many teenage mothers have to drop out of high school after childbearing, they may lack job skills, making it hard for them to find and keep jobs. Finally, teenage mothers may become financially dependent on their families or on welfare. It is common to see very young mothers living home with their babies. In addition, many grandparents are raising children while teenage mothers work to support their children.

There are many ways to control and prevent the occurrence of teenage pregnancy. First, sex education should be taught in school and this education should include information about contraception_ Second, because parents are a child's earliest models of sexuality and they always communicate nonverbally with their children about sex and • sexual values, parents and their children should talk together about sexuality; however, most parents are extremely uncomfortable doing so. Third, the availability of contraceptives and family planning clinics providing birth control services should be promoted to teenagers and adults.

Nevertheless, the control of teenage pregnancy is now unsuccessful, even though we have most of the knowledge and resources needed to solve this problem.

Birth to Unmarried Women By Race of Child and Age of Mother[44]

Race of child and age of mother	1990	1995	1998	1999	2000
Number (1,000) Total live births					
White	647	785	821	840	866
Black	473	421	421	417	427
Under 15 years	11	11	9	9	8
15 to 19 years	350	376	381	374	369
20 to 24 years	404	432	460	476	504
25 to 29 years	230	229	243	247	255
30 to 34 years	118	133	125	125	130
35 to 39 years	(NA)	60	61	63	65
40 years and over	(NA)	13	14	14	16

We need the cooperation from many elements of society: parents, the churches, the schools, state and local legislatures and government agencies. Most people agree about the importance of reproductive health services and research for teenagers,

---

[44] U.S. Census Bureau, Statistical Abstract of U_S.; Births to Unmarried Women By Race of Child and Age mnther. 2002

but there is not yet the willingness to pay the costs for such programs in most, comrnunities of the nation_ There are many aspects to the family that could affect sexual behavior. Teenagers from lower income families are more apt to be sexually active than teenagers from middle or upper income families. Youths from low income families, whether urban ghettos or rural areas, often become sexually active at a younger age and are at a greater risk of an early pregnancy.

Youth living in poor neighborhoods surrounded by teenage pregnancies and unwed single parents are themselves more likely to become sexually active at an earlier age than friends who live in more prosperous neighborhoods. The more brothers and sisters present, the more likely there will be an older sister or brother who is sexually active before marriage, which may serve as a role model for young brothers or sisters_

Both boys and girls who failed to get along with their parents and experienced less parental influence were more apt to experience sexual activities earlier than their peers whose parents were more compatible and exerted greater influence upon them.

Youth are often challenged by "dares" from peers to engage in risk taking behavior and about one-third actually engage in the dare whatever it may be. In 1960, teens rated peers third after their parents and teachers. In 1980, teens rated them first. Girls indicated that they felt social pressure to become sexually active while boys said they felt less pressure. Young women ages 15-19 indicating that religion was important to them, and who attended church regularly were less likely to have reported sexual experiences.

The higher the level of achievement in school and the desire to go to college, the lower the teenager's probability of any sexual activity before age P. Thirty-seven percent of students with grades between C and F en-gaged in sexual activities; 25 percent of those with averages between B and B—were sexually active; and 21 percent of students achieving in the B+, to A range were sexually active. Teenage girls who experienced academic problems, low academic scores, and dropout have a much greater risk of becoming pregnant than girls not experiencing them.

Churches Helping in the Community

When people discuss "faith based community development," they often jump directly into a conversation on the special role of faith based groups, assuming that the meanings of "community" and "development" are well-defined, universally understood and constant. They may even think, given the recent surge of black church participation in the fields of housing and economic development, that faith based community development is • something new, but if we take into account the changing historical understandings of "community" and "development" among black churches, we see that these institutions have figured prominently in African American community development for more than two centuries.

There has never existed a homogeneous black community or a universal black church to defend it. Nor has there ever been a universally accepted understanding of "development." The history of black church-based community development is a history of diverse institutions, championing a kaleidoscopic variety of African American concerns, which themselves have been rooted in broader political, social, and economic contexts that are always shifting.

Throughout slavery, blacks formed religious congregations in secret At that time, the size and composition of black communities were, to a large extent, dictated by the whims of the plantation slave system and faith based development meant fighting the great absurdity of slavery with ideas and concrete acts of resistance. It meant among other things, presenting blacks as full humans, beloved of God and central protagonists in the divine drama of history, not as sub-humans alien to God and godliness.

Churches often pull people together around common ethnicity, regional or national origin, class background, political. orientation, life stage, or lifestyle. Less often, congregations form around shared neighborhood identity. Many churches draw membership from a geographic area much wider than the immediate neighborhood. People choose churches according to social identity more than spatial proximity. One black congregation then might primarily consist of educated middle-class professionals, while another consists of working poor people. One church may attract southern migrants, while another appeals mainly to native northerners. Another church might serve Haitians or West Indians rather than blacks born in the United States. None of these churches need be located where their target populations live as long as the church is not too far away. People will "commute" to worship where they feel at home. This is why we sometimes see solid middle-class black churches located in poor black neighborhoods.

Community development groups that organize across neighborhoods are promising in this regard. Such groups take best advantage of the way many churches think of themselves and their network-building activities as locally based, but not neighborhood focused. Rather than focusing entirely on one neighborhood or another, these initiatives can highlight the common plight of multiple poor neighborhoods and challenge undesirable urban policies. At the same time, such groups can encourage churches to notice and become active in immediate neighborhood affairs. This may be an especially useful way to pull wealthier "commuter" churches into the struggles of the poor areas where they sometimes locate.

What did God do for you and me when we became Christians? He gave us dignity and responsibilities in addition to eternal life. As a result, we are called to treat others the same way. We want to help give neighbors/neighborhoods and communities HOPE (Helping Obtain Purposeful Existence) through a relationship with Jesus. God wants that kind of change, but our neighborhoods are not what God intended. God has shown us how to live and has told us how to achieve those ideals. His goal is to restore us to our original identity as children reflecting His image, to our original vocation as productive stewards, and to our living together in just and peaceful relationships.

God expects Christians as disciples of Jesus to cause positive change in the entire human life, materially, socially, and spiritually, and to find a Life of enjoyment in Him. God uses gifted, equipped, empowered, and mandated Christians to accomplish those purposes. Christians declare the gospel by life, by word, and by deed. We are the message through our life in Christ, displayed by all we say and do. God's redemptive work is not only in the spiritual realm but all of life lived before God.

In creation, we see what was meant to be, but because of the fall we see what is working against us. Through redemption in Jesus, however, we see what we can be, and by His Spirit, we know who and what can help us get there.

Faith Based Organizations to Help Juveniles

By removing the barriers, Faith Based Organizations create the opportunity for religious groups to apply for government contracts and grants or to be eligible to accept vouchers to provide—certain services, but first government welfare and other agencies have to decide what services they should purchase. After officials have decided what to buy and how much money to give out, then a public notice is published, announcing that the government is looking for suppliers of those services. These organizations make it possible for all kinds of religious organizations, along with other groups, to compete to become a chosen supplier.

Sometimes officials will announce what needs they seek to meet, leaving it up to nonprofit organizations and others to propose how they would respond to the problems if they won the funding. In any case, it is up to the government officials to decide what funds are available and what services should be purchased. This opens the door to allow formerly excluded groups to compete. It does not create a special fund just for religious groups and it does not create any right for faith based organizations to get government funding.

Even before Charitable Choice was put into the first federal law in 1988, different government programs to fund homeless shelters, job training, or work with at-risk juveniles have had different rules about which organizations are eligible for funding and under what conditions. Sometimes those rules have been flexible or have been applied flexibly, so that organizations with a clear religious character have been able to take part along with secular nonprofits. In other cases, the rules are extremely restrictive. Sometimes the price of government funds has been the requirement that religious organizations must remove all religious symbols from their facilities or agree no longer to insist that employees must agree to the organization's faith statement and standards.

Faith based organizations clear up confusion, stop governments from discriminating against religious groups when it makes funding decisions, and puts in the law-specific protections for the religious character of groups that accept government money. This is a very significant advance in religious freedom and carries the promise of new opportunities for faith-based organizations to serve as allies with government.

Baltimore Rising, is one faith based program, molded on successful youth violence reduction initiatives in Philadelphia and Boston, which focuses on the 100 most at risk youth across three city districts—East, West, and Northwest—and takes a twofold approach to outreach. The first is a mentoring initiative, which will connect at risk youth with 300 mentors from across city neighborhoods, churches and government. The estimated cost to run such a program is charted below:[45]

ANNUAL BUDGET

10 Youth workers	$300,000
Training	$10,000
10 Volunteer Coordinators	$50,000
Communications (5 radio/phones/ w/annual service)	$3,250
Youth Incentives (activities, fees, food, etc., 100 youths)	$10,000
Vehicle Operating Costs (gas mileage, 1, 000 per employee)	$1,600
Insurance	$2,500
Total Per Cluster	$377,350
3 Clusters (Western, Eastern, Northwestern)	$1,132,050
Tracking, Evaluation and Capacity Building – Public/private Ventures, University of Pennsylvania	$90,000
TOTAL BUDGET	$1,222,050

---

[45]   Baltimore Rising, City of Baltimore. Press Advisory Release 2/13/01.

Conclusion/Summary

The reason why I have such a personal interest in writing about black youth and the Juvenile Justice System is because as a minister in the inner city, I deal with a lot of young people who are just looking for love. They are starving for attention that they do not receive in their homes or their schools. The teachers do not have the sufficient amount of time to render special attention to each individual that may be in need of special services. While ministering to a great deal of these black youth I find many of them live in fatherless homes. They may not have a mother, and this leaves other adults raising them or most of them are on the streets unsupervised.

It is my opinion that a lot of these youth have been deprived of opportunities that life may have offered them had their situation been different. They were given an unfair change like other young men who are in the juvenile detention centers. I realize that we cannot change time, but life can be lived a lot differently and much easier. When we know for a fact that someone loves us, it makes a huge difference in our actions and decision-making.

We can clearly see what the problem is, and it is about time we found a solution. It is about time we provide some type of positive answers to our young people. It is time that we stood accountable for our future_ There are many reasons why I choose this topic. I have a deep passion for a fallen humanity, to see the lost saved and the downtrodden lifted up. You see, I know firsthand about juveniles, simply because at one time in my life I was a troubled youth. Thus, I understand what it is to be rejected, to be let down and disappointed. know what it is to hang out with the wrong friends and to skip school_

Children become a product of their environment and their surroundings and it is about time we change the pictures that they see.

History as we know it teaches us that finding solutions to youth violence, as for all human problems, will not be easy and it will certainly not be done overnight. There is a little consensus among officials that we have put in office about the most effective way to curb violence. While some officials are in favor of the get tough policies, others are in agreement with the rehabilitative programs_

As you have read this report, it was intended to suggest that there are in fact many promising strategies and programs that would reduce and treat youth violence_ You can also see that all youth are not bad they are just misled_ However, with early intervention of violent behavior patterns we will better equip ourselves with the knowledge of how to deal with these individuals on a one on one level.

Youth violence may be more difficult to understand today than at any other period in history. Reduction in violent offenses will certainly offer hope during this time when the nature of American youth violence is changing_ At one time the youth violence was common only in inner-city neighborhoods; violence has spread to rural and suburban neighborhoods and schools.

My only hope is that this paper served a positive purpose and offered useful solutions to an ongoing problem. Before we can ever attempt to move forward to that day when our young people are free from drugs and violence, we must go back and restore that which one day was lost. We sat back and let the officials and politicians take prayer out of school and we allowed the devil to move in on our most precious possession, our young people. There is no more time to waste in legislation and in politicians who are not willing to make a difference. The time is now.

We must realize that as Christians, we must be willing to help these troubled children. If not, we will always be haunted by the fact that we could help them and did nothing_ This particular subject is indeed and should be constant threat to us. It is just like Satan it clings to our every word and action. The oppressor of our young people watches us constantly in hopes that we will invite him back into our own lives.

His demeanor is strategically tactful and clever. He awaits the opportunity to step in and take control over our young people_ This man never walks away and he never gives up_ However, we as Christians must remain strong for our young people_ We know the telltale signs of what direction our children are headed in and more importantly we are familiar with mindset. Even though, we are conscious of what is happening, the best thing we can do is stand by them and continue to pray for them. You may ask yourself, "Where do we go from here?" The process by which violence is taught is circular. It begins in the family, expanding through the culture of the—larger society in which a child grows and matures and then again is reinforced or discouraged in the family.

When parents demean and strike each other or their children, when children are encouraged to be bullies or fight back on the playground, and when they have easy access to real or toy guns and other weapons, violence is being taught. When stereotypes and prejudice frame interactions with people who are different from us, the scene is being set for violence. Glorifying war and relishing violence in competitive sports may reinforce violent behavior. When violence and sexual aggression are combined in the media, in song lyrics, in multimedia computer games, and in the vernacular, the message of violence (including sexual assault) is reinforced.

The process by which violence is taught is circular. It begins in the family, expanding through the culture of the larger society in which a child grows and matures and then again is reinforced or discouraged in the family. The search for ways to help children. learn more appropriate behaviors requires a close look at institutional practices, public policies, and media programming that perpetuate violent attitudes, images, and behaviors.

Bibliography

Administration on Children, Youth and Families (2002). Child Maltreatment 2000. Washington, D.C.: U.S. Department of Health & Human. Services.

Amnesty International, Report 2000. *Justice on Trial, Chapter VT. p_3.* Previously issued to President Clinton includes the inquiry into complaints of widespread sexual abuse of inmates at the Cluvanna Correctional Center, 2000.

Baltimore Rising, City of Baltimore. Press Advisory Release 2/13/01.

Battin, S., Abbott, K.G. and Catalano, R_ *Criminology.* 1998, 36(1): 93-115.

Centers for Disease Control and Prevention. *National Vital Statistics Reports, VOL 48, No. 11, Table 8.* July 2000.

Cornell, D.G. *What Works in Youth Violence Prevention.* Charlottesville, VA: Curry School of Education, University of Virginia.

Flynn, Kevin. *State Cites Racial Inequality in New York Police Searches.* New York Times. December 1999, at 22.

Guggenheim, Martin_ *Paternalism, Prevention, and Punishment: Pretrial Detention of Juveniles.* New York University Law Review, 52:1064-1092.

Hatcher, Candy. *And Justice For Some.* Seattle Post-intelligencer, April 2000.

Holzer, Harry J. Chief Economist. U.S. Department of Labor; testimony before the U.S_ Commission on Civil Rights. April 16, 1999.

Horn, Wade F. *National Father Initiative, Missing Fathers Take Big* Toll. Montgomery Advertiser, Decmeber 1997.

Human Rights Watch *Interview with LaMont Flanagan,* Commissioner, Division of Pretrial Detention and Services, Maryland Department of Public Safety and Correctional Services, Baltimore, Maryland 5/11/99.

Human Rights Watch. *Racism, Racial Discrimination, Xenophobia and All Forms of Discrimination;* written statement submitted 1999.

Kaiser Family Foundation, *Kids & Media @ the New Millennium* (Nov. 1999): 9, 12.

Kids and Guns. *Juvenile Offenders and Victims: 1999 IVational Report_*

Kopel, David. *Massing the Medium: Analyzing and Responding to media Violence Without Harming the First Amendment, Kansas Journal of Law and Public Policy.* March 2000.

ME. Rev. State Ann. Title 12, 7 1 01(a), (West Supp. 1196).

National Center for State Courts_ Survey entitled, *"How the Public Views State Courts."* Executive Summary, p.2. 1999.

Noguera, Pedor. *Responding to the Crisis Confronting Black Youth: Part 2.* In Motion, page 3.

Office of Juvenile Justice and Delinquency Prevention. *Easy Access to Juvenile Court Statistics: 1988-1997.* (1999).

Osofsky, Joy D. *Children In A Violent Society.* New York: Guilford Press, 1997.

Richissin, T. *Race Predicts handling of Many Young Criminals: Care vs. Punishment of mentally 111 Youth Correlates with Color_* The Baltimore Sun (June 25, 1999), p. IA.

Rohner, Ronald P. and Veneziano, Robert A. *The Importance of Father Love: History and Contemporary Evidence.* Review of General Psychology 5.4 (December 2001): 382-405.

S., James (not his actual name). *Interview in the Montgomery County Detention Center,* July 30, 1999.

Smoler, Mark. *Building Blocks for Youth for A Fair and Effective Youth Justice System.* Youth Law Center, President and spokesperson.

Snyder, H. N. and Sicicmund, M. *Juvenile Offenders and Victims: 1999 National Report.* U.S. Department of Justice, Office of Justice Programs, Office of Juvenile Justice and Delinquency Prevention_

Soler, Mark I. Remarks before the Senate Youth Violence Subcommittee; Senate Judiciary Committee, on the core requirements of the Juvenile Justice Act and the Violent Juvenile and Repeat Offender Act of 1997. Washington, D.C.

Statement of Justice O'Connor to The American Bar Association *on Perceptions of the US. Justice System in 1999,* as reported in The Washington Post (May 16, 1999).

Taylor, T. K. and Biglan, A. *Behavioral Family Interventions for Improving Childrearing: A Review of the Literature for Clinicians and Policy* Makers. Clinical Child and Family Psychology Review 1998; (1): 41-60.

U.S. Census Bureau_ *Statistical Abstract of U.S.; Births to Unmarried Women by Race of Child and Age of Mother.* 2002.

U. S_ Department of Justice. *Accessibility of Firearms and the Use of Firearms By or Against Juveniles. Office of Juvenile Justice and Delinquency Prevention.* Washington, D.C. 2000.

U.S. Department of Labor. *Bureau of Labor Statistics, Occupational Outlook Handbook, 2002-03 Edition, Probation Officers and Correctional Treatment Specialists.*

Washburn, Jennifer. *The At Risk Youth Industry.* The Atlantic Monthly, December 2002.

Zirnring, Franklin E—*American Youth Violence.* New York: Oxford University Press, [998.

VITA

NAME: REV. ANDRE HUIVIPEIREY

ADDRESS: 924 N. PAYSON STREET BALTIMORE, MARYLAND 21223

IN CANDIDACY FOR: MASTER OF DIVINITY

DATE OF BIRTH: 9/5/56

MAJOR:	THEOLOGY
MINOR:	CHRISTIAN EDUCATION
EDUCATION:	

1974	Graduated from Lake Clifton High School Baltimore, Maryland
1988	Delaware Valley School of Trades (D.V.S.T.) Diploma—with Honors/Certificate of Completion Certification in Building Renovation
2000	Graduated from United Baptist College & Seminary Bachelor of Arts Degree in Theology
2001	Johns Hopkins University—School of Professional Studies in Business Education Certificate in Business Administration
2003.	Maryland Eastern Theological Seminary Graduate May, 2003—Master of Divinity